IL BUCO

STORIES & RECIPES

DONNA LENNARD with JOSHUA DAVID STEIN
Photography by GENTL & HYERS
Foreword by ALICE WATERS

HARPER
DESIGN

An Imprint of HarperCollinsPublishers

For Joe and Joaquin

RECIPES

CLOCKWISE FROM TOP LEFT: Alberto Galluffo and Alberto Avalle, Trapani; Catania market, Sicily; Donna, Catania fish market; tablescape, Bottega il Buco, Ibiza; Renato Brancaleoni, cheesemaker; roasted peppers; cleaning porcinis; pasta

Foreword by Alice Waters

I first came to il Buco nearly twenty years ago, and from the moment I entered I felt like I was slipping into a place I'd always known and loved. The lovingly worn big wooden tables, the low golden lighting, the mismatched chairs, the antiques in the corners, the vintage plates and bowls tucked onto shelves—everything about the atmosphere felt inviting, wonderfully idiosyncratic, and deeply personal. And then, the food! From the very beginning, I loved how the cooks were sourcing and making their food: with ripe, seasonal ingredients, simply and skillfully prepared so that the true flavors shone through.

It has been a joy watching the il Buco community grow and evolve in organic and beautiful ways through the years. Over the course of the past two decades, Donna Lennard and il Buco have become integral parts of the Chez Panisse family. Chefs who have worked at Chez Panisse have found a home cooking at il Buco, and the people cooking at il Buco have become close friends and collaborators through the years. Former Chez Panisse chef Christopher Lee helped to open Alimentari in 2011, and I love knowing I can always go there for truly authentic Italian pasta, a great glass of wine, and some of the finest salumi in America. In this book, you will find delicious recipes from all these extraordinary il Buco chefs: Ignacio Mattos, Jody Williams, Sara Jenkins, Justin Smillie, and more.

Il Buco's culinary ethos has always been to do a thing simply, but perfectly—and every endeavor of Donna's is defined by that attention to purity, simplicity, tradition, and provenance. How rare it is to find a restaurant that can let the aliveness and beauty of its ingredients truly speak for themselves. I think it's something that people recognize and respond to instantly. I love that Donna has always understood the vital importance of the people who grow our food and take care of the land, and the chefs who have passed through the teaching grounds of il Buco all understand this too. Last spring, Donna and I walked through the Union Square Greenmarket together, picked ingredients that were ripe and in season, and cooked a meal at Alimentari with my friend David Tanis, longtime Chez Panisse chef and longtime il Buco neighbor. That meal we made together was a celebration of our shared philosophies about food and life—and a celebration of the passionate, creative, ever-growing community that has defined a quarter century of il Buco. You can feel that spirit alive and thriving here in these pages.

LEFT: Donna and Alice, Union Square Greenmarket

OUR STORY

Ask anyone who's been to il Buco, and they'll tell you that it isn't a place, it is a feeling, a feeling of warmth, of home, of ease, and of love, which has only grown over the last twenty-five years.

Crossing the uneven cobblestones and entering the rickety, turn-of-the-century wooden doors, one has the sense of being transported across the Atlantic into another world. Time seems both to stand still and to speed up here. It isn't uncommon to wander out onto Bond Street at half past midnight after a full meal and swear you had walked in but a few minutes before. And it's possible to do this month after month, year after year, until acquaintances become friends and friends become family.

The road that led me to il Buco is long and meandering. I was born in New York City and raised in Chappaqua. My dad traded in metals, and my mom stayed at home, raising me and my two sisters. Our early family dinners were classic midcentury

America: plates of spaghetti with ketchup, 1-2-3 Jell-O, Kraft mac and cheese. We were entranced by the occasional TV dinner. My parents split when I was six, and when I was ten my mom remarried and got serious in the kitchen. She immersed herself in cooking classes and whipped up hors d'oeuvres of spanakopita, shrimp toasts, and chicken cordon bleu à la Julia Child. Having the family around the table was what mattered most, both at home with my mom and stepfather, and at my dad's home in Connecticut, where I spent most weekends with him, my stepmother, and my stepsister.

Though life in Chappaqua was suburban, my horizons were wide. In my preteen years, my dad lived in New York City and exposed us girls to every-

LEFT: Alberto and Donna, Bond Street, 1994 (Donna Lennard's personal archive)

thing the city had to offer. But it wasn't until I traveled to Italy at seventeen, for six weeks with the Putney Exchange, that I had one of those extraordinary experiences that shifted everything for me. I was matched with a lovely Sardinian family in Cagliari, the capital of the beautiful Mediterranean island of Sardinia. There were several other Americans living in the neighboring homes with their Italian "siblings," and we spent our days frolicking in the Mediterranean or sharing stories over long delicious meals from one home to the other. My Italian "sister," Maria, lived with her mother and father in a modest home on the outskirts of the city, where fresh pasta was rolled out each morning, and the aroma of home-cooked tomato sauce wafted through the house daily with the summer breeze. Outside there was a small garden with a handful of apricot and fig trees and the shimmer of early peaches.

It was there that I tasted my very first fresh fig, plucked from those trees. This ripe blast of sweet, succulent flavor shook my world—I was mesmerized. There in this simple garden, feeling the warmth of the sun, surrounded by this wonderful family and new friends I had grown attached to, I felt inducted into a world completely apart from the one in which I had grown up. It uncovered a new part of myself that had nothing to do with who I had been or where I came from. I felt totally at home.

For a long while, I kept those memories packed away, along with the photographs and souvenirs of my time in Sardinia. I moved to New York, attended graduate film school at NYU, fell in love with a fellow film student named Joe Rosato, became a filmmaker, got engaged, and prepared to start a life with Joe after eight beautiful years together. Cagliari belonged to the past.

In 1992, three days before our wedding, Joe lost all feeling in one side of his body. I rushed him to St. Vincent's Hospital in the West Village where he was able to check himself in as if nothing had happened. Thirty minutes later, he suffered a seizure; it was a brain aneurysm. He was in a coma for two days. On the second evening, Joe's family and I were sent home to let him rest and were gathered for dinner at our local restaurant when my phone rang calling me back to the hospital. I only had to glance at my mother's face at the door of the ICU to know that I had lost the love of my life. Joe was thirty-three years old. Our friends and family who flew in for the wedding came instead to a memorial service. Joe was a brilliant filmmaker, a sincere and driven storyteller. He was an unrelenting questioner and selfless listener. We were partners in life and partners in our work. With his death, the plans and dreams we had laid out for our lives were whisked away overnight. I buoyed myself with our two amazing families and began to rebuild my life. I immersed myself in the task of producing the screenplay Joe had recently completed and worked in restaurants to pay the rent on our Tribeca loft. In spite of the indescribable pain of loss, I was determined to live a life for the two of us.

Almost a year later, still adrift, I walked into Arqua restaurant to pick up a bartending gig. Within days, I had fallen for a charismatic figure flying through the room. He had angular features, eyebrows as expressive as calligraphy, and a face lifted from a Caravaggio. Alberto Avalle was officially a waiter at Arqua. But the reality was that he was the spirit of the restaurant. He moved about the dining room with the grace and charm of someone in whose blood flowed the necessity of creating a seamless spectacle of the dining experience. Seconds after the host dropped the menus, Alberto would scoop them back up and guide the guests through his own interpretation of what their meal should be. Dishes soon arrived at the table in perfect harmony. The guests adored him. So did I.

It was *l'amour fou*. We met for trysts in the wine vault and snatched kisses by the drink pass. He eventually moved in with me to help me carry the Tribeca rent until the lease expired, then we moved across the city to a small, sweet apartment in Alphabet City.

Alberto was not an easy partner—he was energetic and quixotic, and mostly unpredictable—and our relationship was more tumultuous than anything I had known. Yet we were somehow connected, and after the loss of Joe, I was determined to hold on to him.

Alberto had been born in Foligno, a small Umbrian town outside Assisi. He grew up tied to the hip of a mystical grandmother who understood the healing power of natural herbs and sold her tinctures in the local market. In his early thirties Alberto became the right hand to a wonderful charismatic chef in central Italy named Angelo Scolastra. At Angelo's side, Alberto was quickly inducted into the intimate secrets of Italian cuisine. It was all about the prime materials. Not unlike Alberto's grandmother, Angelo was a master of nature and knew exactly where to go to find her gifts. When he wasn't hunting wild boar or *uccelli* (tiny sparrowlike birds) or gathering mushrooms, wild asparagus, fennel pollen, and the like, he was locating the freshest artisan-made olive oils and vinegars and planting everything one could think of in his garden. Alberto had started as a waiter in Angelo's Spello restaurant, but soon found himself assisting in every task Angelo could fathom. Over time Angelo, his wife Sandra, and daughter Luisa would build Villa Roncali, an inn with one of the most renowned restaurants in Foligno, and Alberto would be forever a part of the inner circle. Years later, so would I.

By the time I met him, Alberto had had a falling out with his family and had forsaken his home country, first for Spain, then the United States. But he brought to our shoebox kitchen an Italian's unbridled passion for food. Alberto was a purist: When he wasn't at Arqua, he combed the city looking for the highest quality olive oil and traipsed around the East Village in search of pecorino pepato. He was certain there was only one way to cook bacalao (filleted and fried, page 26) and one way to make octopus (*pulpo a la gallega*, page 41). In our tiny one-bedroom apartment with a working fireplace, we began our own little culinary odyssey, roasting wild mushrooms and grilling steak over the fire, letting our tomatoes boil in the pasta water to lose their skins for our *pasta al pomodoro*, watching cockles click open for *pasta con le vongole*, and doubling over with laughter as Alberto polished off an entire loaf of bread slathered in Nutella. These early memories became the marrow of il Buco.

But even though he flourished in it, Alberto was determined to get out of the restaurant business. He saw an exit strategy in antiques. He dreamed of opening an export business—his idea was to find and export the Americana that littered the East Coast farmlands back to Europe. Soon we were tooling around rural Pennsylvania in an old Suzuki Samurai, picking up treasure after treasure at antiques sales and estate auctions, returning across Route 78 with antiques tied to the roof. Our home became overrun with hundred-year-old furniture, our closets stuffed with Pennsylvania Dutch quilts. Market scales hung from the ceiling, corners were crammed with century-old tricycles and radios from the 1940s and '50s. Old toboggans were mounted on the walls.

One day, while I was rattling the cobblestones of Bond Street in the Suzuki, I saw two fantastical chandeliers hanging in the window of number 47, glimmering like beacons in the grime. I pulled over immediately, intrigued. Bond Street wasn't like it is today; it still felt a little bit wild and deserted, especially on the street level. The only business on the block was Bob the Furniture Guy, who ran a kiosk on the corner of Lafayette selling antiques. Carefully avoiding the crack vials littering the sidewalk, I made my way inside. The space was being used as an artist's workshop. The floors were painted a deep dark brown of many coats. The walls were white and spattered with the clay of the kilns in the middle of the room. Powdery white sculptures lined the shelves. The walls in the front ten feet of the space, however, were painted in a harlequin burgundy and gold pattern with an unusual inscription above: BEING THERE WAS LIKE BEING IN A STRANGE MUSEUM. I WAS AN OBJECT ON THE SHELF LIKE ALL THE OTHER OBJECTS.

FOLLOWING, CLOCKWISE FROM TOP LEFT: Original sign, 1994 (Donna Lennard's personal archive); il Buco wine cellar; chef's pass; table 8A (Gentl & Hyers); Bond Street; Alberto and Donna, 1996 (Donna Lennard's personal archive); Warren Muller chandelier; bar; anchovies; Ricardo (Gentl & Hyers); Cesar; cheese and pastry; Roberto, wine cellar (Thibault Jeansen); figs; Hasib; interior; La Banda dell Buco (Donna Lennard's personal archive; all other photographs: Michael Grimm)

I introduced myself to the three artists who shared the space. As we began to get acquainted, I discovered that the group was in a dispute with their landlord, who wanted to raise their rent from $1,750 to $2,000 for the ample 2,000-square-foot space. They had been looking to rent out the back room in order to make ends meet. What a coincidence that Alberto and I were looking for a space to begin our export business. After my promise to bring my boyfriend the next day to see the space, Warren Muller, one of the artists, placed a gold-leaf-painted apple in my hand.

I sped home and dragged Alberto back the next day. He didn't even have to enter to know this was the right space for us. Outside the store was a large sheet of wood, painted with gold leaf on both sides, with a perfectly round hole about a foot in diameter cut out in the center. "Il Buco," he said, gazing at the sign. This was the name of the fort in which he had raised hell with his friends growing up in Umbria. The name also harkened back to his all-time favorite Vittorio Gassman/Marcello Mastroianni film, *I Soliti Ignoti—Big Deal on Madonna Street* in English—a 1958 Italian comedy caper that tells the story of *La Banda del Buco*, a group of hard-up small-time thieves who, deciding to rob a pawn shop, drill a hole in the wall next door but end up in the neighbor's kitchen instead and raid the fridge. Alberto must have seen the film a hundred times. We walked inside and felt the energy in the floorboards, the walls, the history buried deep within the wine cellar below. From day one Alberto was sure this space was protected by our dearest guardian angels, his "nonna" and my Joe. And that has never changed.

The artists moved to Philadelphia, and the space was ours. Joe's brother, Michael, a gifted muralist, swooped in to assist and together we painted the walls, while our dear neighbor Todd Nickey sanded the floors. We filled the rooms with American primitive furniture, wooden chairs in all sorts of colors, farm tables, the vintage radios and railroad lanterns from our apartment. We prepared our own midday *pranzo* (lunch) each afternoon and our clients joined us for a glass of wine or a slice of prosciutto. We knew that what we were selling wasn't just furniture but an experience. We wanted il Buco to be so welcoming our customers couldn't bear to leave and, if they did, they'd take a little bit of il Buco with them.

What better way to achieve this—and loosen them up—than with some booze and snacks? We applied for a wine and beer license, which arrived on Alberto's fortieth birthday. In order to convince our landlords, Steve and Jerry—a pair of old-school New York guys— to allow us to operate an eating and drinking establishment inside our store, we invited them to lunch. They'd never seen anything like il Buco and hadn't imagined they ever would on Bond Street. Alberto, at his most charming, seated them at a large farm table in the middle of the room, served a head-on prawn pasta, and opened a bottle (and another and another) of wine. Stunned by the transformation of the space, and bowled over by the meal, they agreed to allow us to run the space as a restaurant. "We'll never be a restaurant," insisted Alberto. "We're a tapas bar with wine, selling antiques!" Jerry and Steve, who had never been to Spain and had no idea what a tapas bar was, shrugged. "Call it whatever you want," they said. "As long as we get to eat here, we're happy."

There are two types of people in the world: people who read manuals and people who don't. I am one of the latter; maybe it's because I'm a Taurus, headstrong but heart-forward, or maybe it's because I'm the daughter of a trader, from back in the day when fortunes were made by hunches. I operate by instinct, move with my gut, lead with my heart. It obviously hadn't occurred to me that il Buco would become my life's work. Young and in love, we just did what felt right. With my filmmaker's eye, Alberto's intuitive sense of design, and our shared aesthetic, we trusted one another implicitly. We never thought we'd be a restaurant. Alberto feared it so much that he called it "the R-word." In his mind, il Buco was still an antiques store. It's just that now we sold not only the farmhouse tables but the farm-fresh food atop them. When the space was set up and ready to open, we stepped outside for a breath of air, looked at one another deeply in the eyes, and said, "Did you ever imagine we would make a space this beautiful?" Together we had created something beyond either of our dreams or expectations. This was the magic we shared, this was il Buco.

When we opened that August, Alberto, who had never before worked as a chef, ran the tiny kitchen with Angelo's voice in his ears. I ran the floor of the dining room with our two partners, Giorgio Cappelletti and Carlo Pulixi, friends from our Arqua days. We were indeed *La Banda del Buco*. The menu was simple both by necessity and choice. It was dictated by Alberto's travels through Spain and his own home country: *bruschetta di pomodori*; *angulas basquas*, frizzled baby eels from the Basque Country in olive oil and garlic; *boquerones*, tender anchovies imported from Galicia; and *Gazpacho a la Andaluz* (page 152).

Though Alberto was a wizard in the kitchen, his technical skills were outstripped by his passion for purity. He moved with a confidence that had nothing to do with textbook training. He knew from his years with Angelo that technique without taste is a waste anyway. We poured all our efforts into making sure all of our ingredients were the best we could find. All of our produce came from the Union Square Greenmarket. We took the Suzuki Samurai and returned to the farmland of Bucks County. But now, instead of hunting for antique farm tools, we returned with smoked legs of lamb and prosciutto. We visited the fish-smoking houses in Great Barrington for freshwater catfish and Maine steelhead and the meat-smoking houses of the Catskills for peppered beef and capocollo. These we sliced and served simply on wooden platters. When our stores ran low, Rick Laakkonen, our dear friend and chef of the River Café across the Brooklyn Bridge, taxied across the river to save the day with an occasional foie gras terrine or homemade soup.

I found that I had a sensitive palate and could almost visualize the flavors I tasted. Together we shared ideas. Alberto brought them into reality in the kitchen while I tended to the guests. Although I sometimes found his fanatic devotion to purity and his quick temper frustrating, we truly had a karmic connection. Everything we touched turned to gold, as Warren's apple had foreshadowed.

Almost immediately, il Buco was a hit. The place was like an oasis on the seemingly deserted block, and the artists and sculptors who occupied the lofts around it began to emerge. Chuck Close, whose studio was on the corner, became an early regular. Soon word spread about this little tapas bar in the middle of this cobblestoned street, and people came from all over. We were indeed a trading post of crafts, cultures, ideas, food, and wine. By now, Bond Street was a mecca of antiques stores and il Buco became a connecting thread. On nice days, we'd drag a small farm table across the street to sit in the sun, drinking Sancerre and sharing Alberto's freshly made pasta with our neighbors Catherine and Annick of CapSud, Stacy of Rhubarb Home, or Sandra and Orhan of Buying the Farm.

But after the covers exceeded fifty, Alberto realized that he was in over his head. A few months in, he fired himself. We both knew we needed a real chef. We found one in Thierry Amezcua, a young chef from Mexico City. Thierry had a natural talent for Mediterranean fare. His food was simple and delicious, and his smile was infectious. His wife, Debbie, eventually joined us as pastry chef, and the business began to take off. Meanwhile, after reading an article about us in *New York* magazine, one of Alberto's childhood friends, Roberto Paris, showed up on our doorstep. He had been drifting between San Francisco and New York, working as an art gallery lighting installer. Like Alberto, Roberto too was living in exile from Foligno. Although he'd been a citizen of the world, living all over Italy and Germany from a young age, dabbling in the wine trade, he had no desire to work in restaurants. Nevertheless, Alberto convinced him to join our team as the sommelier. Our boutique wine list—a mix of personal favorites from Spain, Italy, and North and South America—began to take shape and develop its own point of view. Roberto championed little-known wines close to his heart, including Sagrantino di Montefalco, a varietal from the hills of Umbria where he and Alberto had grown up.

After the first couple of years, il Buco stabilized, and Alberto and I were free to travel. We traveled to Spain and Portugal, up to Alberto's beloved Galicia, across the coast to Finesterra, literally the end of the continent, down to Porto and south to Lisbon, and across to Ronda and Jerez. Our menu was inspired by these memorable visits. In the port of Cedeira, the first taste of *percebes* (goose barnacles), *angulas* (eels, page 42), or the hundreds of different crustaceans coming out of that cold Galician Atlantic; the first Albariño and Manzanilla; the first jamon Iberico. My life was expanding in every direction. Perhaps this is what kept me going through the more challenging times of our increasingly turbulent relationship.

Once Alberto reconnected with Roberto, it was only a matter of time before he did so with his family as well. In 1997, Alberto and I headed to Italy for a whirlwind tour. Returning to the country with Alberto was a revelation. He introduced me to vineyards and to *frantoi*, or olive oil mills, where we watched Moraiolo olives being ground into paste and then pressed into the golden liquid we drizzled over warm, garlic-rubbed bread topped with salt. We visited *saline*, or salt fields, in Sicily and walked among sweet-smelling *batterie* in Modena, barrels full of grape must on its way to becoming the famous balsamic vinegar. We wended our way through the Umbrian countryside, stopping at every osteria and trattoria we could find.

On one visit, we sped from the north of Sardinia on Alberto's bright yellow BMW R1100S moto, stopping to visit a bottarga producer in Oristano, then south to Cagliari. There I reconnected with my host family

from fifteen years earlier, in the same house with the same garden; everything intact. The meal we shared that day around the table was a homecoming I will never forget. With Maria, and her now quite aged parents and extended family around the table, I could feel my worlds connecting across time and space.

We returned to New York inspired. We began building relationships with producers in Italy like Marco Pandolfi, who turns his silvery olives into a delicious grassy olive oil (see page 81), and with Salvatore Daidone, a salt maker in Sicily (see page 139). That same passion that sent Alberto roaming the city for our fireplace dinners now stretched across the ocean and resulted in the creation of the il Buco trilogy, our own line of olive oil, salt, and vinegar. In 1998, we found a new young chef, Jody Williams, who had staged at Caffe Arti e Mestieri in Reggio Emilia and who shared our passion for Italian cuisine. Soon she came aboard and tilted the menu from Spain to Italy. It was the first of many transitions in the life of il Buco and mine as well.

After Alberto reestablished his bridge to Italy, we continued to cross it often, sometimes together, but more often separately. For a little while we tried to make our relationship work from a distance, but by 2001, the combination of the day-to-day stresses of the restaurant and the day-to-day tumult between us was too much. One day, after more than nine years together, he decided to return to Italy for good. In some ways this was devastating. I had lost a life and business partner yet again. In another way, Alberto's exit opened up a path for me to grow.

With Alberto gone, il Buco became my charge. Of course, Alberto was—and is still—an inspiration, constantly bearing new products, ideas, and his over-the-top energy. But I was quickly discovering my own voice and learning to trust my own instincts.

From day one, il Buco's philosophy had been to source the best prime materials and to do the least possible to create the best result. This would never change. It takes just the right kind of chef to pull it off,

RIGHT: Donna with Vita partners Antonello and Lorenzo Radi FOLLOWING, CLOCKWISE FROM TOP LEFT: sample menu; Harding Aldonzar; salumi board; Chef Christopher Lee; Tiki Thiam, Chef Joel Hough, Chef Jody Williams, and Harding Aldonzar; olive oil tasting; Chef Roger Martinez; razor clams (Gentl & Hyers), Chef Joel Hough; kale salad; Chef Ignacio Mattos; seared octopus; Chef Sara Jenkins (Gentl & Hyers); fava beans (Gentl & Hyers); pasta; Chef Justin Smillie (all other photographs: Michael Grimm)

a product whisperer who possesses the knowledge and restraint needed to extract from each raw ingredient its most delicious essence. The approach is as simple as it is unforgiving.

Since I am not a chef, I see my role as something between a navigator, a philosopher, a creative director, and most important, a talent scout. It's my job to find chefs whose philosophies align with il Buco. I spend the first few months of a new chef's reign tethered to the kitchen, but as soon as they're up and running, I slowly back myself out the door. I serve as a sounding board for their ideas, they blossom, and il Buco evolves in inexplicable ways. This collaboration is my deepest joy.

More than fifteen chefs have passed through il Buco in the last quarter century. Many have gone on to open restaurants of their own. Chefs like Jody Williams, Sara Jenkins, Ignacio Mattos, Justin Smillie, Joel Hough, and a host of other great talents all played parts in the life of il Buco and, quite honestly, many still do. Under Jody's tenure we established our true connection to Italy with house-made pasta (page 180), chicken livers with rosemary, and roasted quail with lardo. Sara Jenkins, who as a diplomat's daughter had grown up in Lebanon and Italy, had an innate sense of all things Mediterranean, and it was with Sara that we initiated our salumi curing program. Ignacio Mattos, a young chef from Uruguay to whom my friend Francis Mallmann introduced me, knew how to take three things, put them on a plate, and make them sing. The kale salad on the menu today (page 159) is untouched from the day Ignacio added it almost fifteen years ago, and it's just as delicious. Justin Smillie possessed the ability to champion each season with robust flavors. It was during his tenure that we earned our highest accolades, buoyed by inventive dishes like octopus with chickpeas (page 107) and the short rib with colatura, celery, and walnuts (page 232). Most recently, at il Buco, Roger Martinez brings his Catalan roots with a myriad of Spanish flavors, merging the restaurant's early Iberian influences with the Italian ones. At Alimentari, Preston Madson highlights diverse flavors from his upbringing in the American South and Mediterranean know-how from his years on the team of chef Jonathan Waxman. The family of il Buco has grown over the years. In pursuit of the highest quality ingredients, I've returned again and again to the vineyards and orchards of Italy and to the fields and farms of upstate New York. Just as I've worked closely with chefs, now I work closely with an ever-growing community of producers who are as much a part of our story as the chefs, our regulars, or I am.

In 2003, I began dating one of my regular customers, a fellow foodie with an acute eye for design and a focus on sustainability. Alejandro and I aligned easily on these common passions. In March of 2005, I gave birth to our son, Joaquin. Though the relationship didn't last, I was lucky to have Roberto and the close-knit il Buco team to give me support. At three months Joaquin began to accompany me on trips back to Italy and his extended family stretched across the Atlantic. The line between my life and that of the restaurant faded even more.

Raising a son on my own, I started to pull back from the day-to-day workings of the restaurant. Yet I still needed to follow the passions of the il Buco family. During these years there were many opportunities for expansion, but none seemed right until we happened upon the old lumberyard on Great Jones Street, exactly a block north of il Buco. With dreams of relaunching our salumi program, which had been shut down by the health department in 2009 (see Salumi chapter, page 205), as well as finding a home for the products Alberto had now begun to package and import as our exclusive il Buco product line, I began work on what would become il Buco Alimentari e Vineria.

At much the same time, my dearest neighbors/regulars at il Buco introduced me to another handsome Italian, this time an entrepreneur turned ski guide from Trento, in the north of Italy: *un trentino*. Though much different from Alberto, Luca pushed

me to realize my vision of Alimentari and tirelessly helped me in its creation. We were married in June of 2010, on the island of Lastovo in Croatia, just before we started construction of the space on Great Jones Street. Joaquin was our ring bearer in a quiet ceremony atop a lighthouse as the sun set over the Mediterranean. A new chapter of my life had begun.

If il Buco was the "living room" for our guests, Alimentari would be the production studio, a place where our clients could take a piece of il Buco home or enjoy all the quality ingredients from our open kitchen in our bright, inviting dining room. It would be a warm, casual restaurant with an active market in the front, supported by a full-scale bakery and salumeria below. With the help of longtime Chez Panisse veteran Christopher Lee, Bernardo Flores, our salumiere, would have an opportunity to present his housemade lardo, guanciale, and capocollo in an HACCP-approved facility. And we would finally have the space to fully realize the bread program we had always dreamed of.

Alimentari marked my own creative venture, the first expansion of il Buco in nearly twenty years. I joined forces with a longtime customer, Ian McPheely and his partner, Christian Garnett, at Grayling, to design the space. It was a hugely ambitious project in need of resources. As serendipity would have it, I met my business partner at a private benefit for Alice Waters held in the early days of her launching Edible Schoolyard in New York. The event was held at David and Monica Zwirner's house, and Alice was there, of course, as were Ignacio and several of the Chez Panisse expats. I was introduced to David and Monica, who were huge fans of il Buco, and a couple months later—over some warm bread, sliced prosciutto, and a bottle of wine—we decided to join forces in creating Alimentari. Its scale and ambition were overwhelming, and I was, frankly, terrified it might not take. That sense of casual freedom that marked the opening of il Buco was long gone. But with Luca to support me and Justin Smillie by my side in the kitchen, we were

blessed with a visit from *New York Times* restaurant critic Pete Wells, who gave us three stars. We were over the moon. With tears of joy in my eyes I read the review to my staff. It felt like we had finally arrived, that I was who I knew I was back in Sardinia, connecting through time and the vagaries of citizenship, to my mother culture.

In some ways, as I reach the twenty-five-year mark of il Buco, everything is coming back full circle. In 2016, two of my dearest friends in Umbria, Antonello and Lorenzo Radi, began to push me to pursue a project we had dreamed of for years—a home line dedicated to artisanal wares from Italy. With Alimentari up and running, they wasted no time sourcing a gorgeous line of products and shipping it over for a trial run. Without quite realizing what was happening, il Buco Vita was born. A rustic loft space became available a couple of doors down on Bond Street, above a scrap metal shop, the only survivor from our early days. We took it. Charlie Raimondo—whom Alberto had threatened to shoot with a BB gun twenty years before if he dropped another barrel of scrap metal on the sidewalk next to our bedroom window—was now my landlord. It was the perfect showroom. With its original floorboards, fireplace, and tin ceiling, the space harkened back to the early days of il Buco and old New York. With Antonello and Lorenzo sourcing artisan objects from their motherland, Vita gave our clients the chance to enhance their own homes with the warm patinas of Italy, and re-create the atmosphere that had made il Buco so inviting.

Alberto's back, too, in his own way, and in a way that works for both of us. Though we never fully lost contact over the years, through his marriage and mine, our lives spun out separately across the ocean, each of us busy with our own children to raise. He continued to source products for il Buco and assist with imports for Alimentari. I'd see him a several times a year over shared meals with friends—our kids in tow—in Italy or New York.

LEFT: Il Buco Alimentari and Vineria exterior, Great Jones Street FOLLOWING, CLOCKWISE FROM TOP LEFT: Bernardo Flores; Alimentari's seasonal fruit crostata and coffee; house-cured salumi; Alimentari's front windows; Olaf at the pass; view of dining room from loft; wine director Roberto Paris in discussion; Brianna Giannizzero refilling bread rack; Alimentari counter (Noe DeWitt); cheese selection, Alimentari (all other photographs: Gentl & Hyers)

Three years ago, my nephew Danny Rubin called me up a week before his college graduation, asking to join the il Buco team. Alberto jumped right in. He took Danny under his wing, imparting that same sense of wide-eyed appreciation of life that bowled me over twenty years ago. The two proved to be kindred spirits. Danny took over the Alimentari counter, collaborating with Alberto across the Atlantic.

A couple of years ago Alberto was in town for our *sagra del maiale*, our annual pig roast. He was living in Foligno at the time and was fed up with the cold Umbrian winters. He had recently received an invitation from a friend to visit him in Ibiza and asked me whether he should take up the offer. "Go," I said, "it's the best time to be there in the off-season." A few weeks later I got a call out of the blue.

"Donna," Alberto said, "I've found it!"

"Found what?"

"Our next il Buco."

I rolled my eyes but heard him out. He had found a charming former *formaggeria* in Santa Gertrudis, on the quiet side of the famous party paradise. "I haven't felt this way in twenty-three years!" he said. "It's magical." I knew enough to trust him on all things magic.

I found out when I visited in late December 2018, that, true to form, he was right. In June, with the help of Danny, we opened Bottega il Buco. It's a laid-back spot where Sicilian ancient grain focaccia emerges fresh from the oven, glistening in the Ibicencan sun, ready to accompany artisan-tinned fish from Spain and Portugal, cured meats and cheeses, or a fresh sliced fish crudo or ceviche. It's a place brimming with locals and tourists alike from morning until night, connecting in Spanish or French or Dutch or English or any combination thereof, over plates of baked fish under salt (page 216) or pasta with squid ink and bottles of cava.

With Bottega, Danny earned his stripes and then some, taking us through the first two seasons with his coattails flying in the wind. Though it is still more work on my plate, Ibiza has provided another bridge across "the pond," this time to a country that has always intrigued me, on an island infused with its own awe and myth: a beautiful sea, the freshest ingredients, and a lovely place to enjoy with my son and friends both old and new. My little piece of Sardinia in Spain. It's il Buco, Spanish style. Alberto and I aren't the same people we were back in 1994. We're both older, grayer, and maybe a little wiser now. But the minute we connected over Bottega, it was as if the years sloughed off, leaving us young again and, as always, hungry.

For twenty-five years I've been guided by a feeling. Now what's right for il Buco is as natural to me as breathing. It's a voice I learned to listen to a long time ago. Like a character in a novel, the spirit of the restaurant guides me more than I guide it. Nothing's been analyzed. Nothing's intellectualized. It hasn't always been an easy road, but it's been a true one. From an indelible loss sprang a new life full of twists and turns. It has brought me a world of friends, family, and food I never could have imagined. Ultimately, it has brought me to myself.

This book contains all il Buco has taught me. At least all I can put into words. It's not simply a collection of recipes for sumptuous easy meals, though it is that. It's not just an appreciation of olive oil, salt, vinegar, and the benedictions of the Mediterranean kitchen, though they are many. It isn't even just a story of the friendship, the love, and the community that sprang up around il Buco, though those connections have changed the trajectory of my life. It's a book about learning to listen to that voice inside you, letting you know exactly who you are, and connecting you with people and cultures that inspire you. It is a celebration of life.

What began with the first bite into a fresh fig in Sardinia has grown into an inspiring way of life, one that feeds me and nourishes me daily, one that I hope to share with you here.

—Donna Lennard, New York City, February 2020

A Readers' Guide

This book is designed to introduce those of you who don't know il Buco to the stories and recipes that have carried us throughout this twenty-five-year journey. For those of you who know us well, we hope you will smile nostalgically as you delve back into the past and recall the food, wine, and moments that endeared il Buco to you.

To give you a sense of the world behind the scenes at the restaurants, we've interspersed the recipes of this book with narrative chapters, including some of our favorite stories about the products, producers, and lifestyle that have inspired us along the way. You'll hear the voices of some of our dearest customers. You'll travel with us across the Atlantic to meet our olive oil, salt, and vinegar producers. You'll discover the secrets behind the world of the bread and salumi we produce at Alimentari. We will showcase the many artisans whose handiwork comes to New York via our homeware line, il Buco Vita. We invite you to explore our Ibicencan outpost, to feast with us at home, and to partake in our annual pig roast on the street in front of the restaurant in celebration of the incredible friends, family, and community to whom we owe twenty-five years of gratitude.

The recipe chapters begin with tapas, inspired by Alberto's Spanish "exile" and our many trips to explore her food, wine, and culture. We continue through the meal with antipasti (both from the sea and the land) toward pane, pizza, and crostini, a sampling of our bread program, and *zuppe e insalate*, soups and salads. That is followed by *primi piatti*, our famous pastas, and hearty *secondi*, our main dishes, with accompanying *contorni*, side dishes. We close the book—and the meal—with the sweet *dolci* with which to cleanse the palate from this multitude of flavors and to leave you with sweet memories of a journey through time and space from old New York across the Atlantic and back.

CLOCKWISE FROM TOP LEFT: Roberto with *Gazzetta dello Sport*, Portonovo, Italy; peaches, Catania market, Sicily; Chef Luisa Scolastra, Villa Roncalli, Foligno; Alimentari window; fresh mackerel; Bertha making pasta; Emanuele in his studio, Marche, Italy; fruit crostatas

TAPAS

———

BACALAO FRITO

Though bacalao, or salt cod, is a staple from the tapas bars of Bilbao to the botequim of Rio de Janeiro, the fish starts in the frigid waters of Newfoundland's Bay of Biscay, and that is where Alberto will send you: to the source. There it is caught, salted, and dried. This was traditionally done on the sides of cliffs—hence the Norwegian name, *klippfish*, or cliff fish—but today the fish is dried in less poetic but more sanitary modern factories.

For the last five hundred years, salt cod has been exported around the world and has taken root everywhere from Greece to Mexico to Italy to Spain. Once at its destination, the fish is rehydrated and desalinated by being soaked in fresh water. Sometimes the bacalao is stewed, but my favorite way to eat it is fried. These two preparations—croquetas de bacalao and bacalao frito—are simple ways to showcase the tender subtle charm of the fish. In the croquetas (found on the next page), the golden crust yields to a soft, creamy, cloudlike filling. A Meyer lemon aioli adds a kick of refreshing citrus. For more straightforward tapas, simple buttermilk-soaked bacalao frito, touched with tarragon and a bit of heat, are like the world's most delicious fish fingers. They are finished perfectly with a squeeze of lemon (or even the aioli from the croquetas recipe).

Serves 4 to 6

1 pound dried bacalao (salt cod)
1 cup all-purpose flour
1 cup semolina flour
2 cups buttermilk
1 teaspoon cracked black pepper
1 teaspoon dried chili flakes
1 tablespoon torn fresh tarragon leaves
Canola oil, for frying
Fine sea salt, for finishing
2 lemons, cut into wedges, for serving
Aioli (optional, page 29)

1. Rehydrate the bacalao by soaking it in a large pot of cold water for 16 to 24 hours in the refrigerator. Change the water at least three times. The longer the fish stays submerged, the less salty it becomes. Once the fish is rehydrated, remove and pat dry. Using a paring knife, carefully remove the pin bones. Slice the fish into strips roughly the size of a finger.

2. Whisk together the flours in a large bowl. In a separate bowl, combine the buttermilk, black pepper, chili flakes, and tarragon.

3. Heat 2½ inches of canola oil in a dutch oven until it reaches 375°F.

4. Dip the bacalao into the buttermilk mixture, then into the flour mixture. Shake to remove excess coating and place in the hot oil, being careful that the pieces do not touch. Fry until golden, flipping once, for about 5 minutes total.

5. Remove the bacalao from the pot with a spider or slotted spoon and place on a paper towel–lined tray. Sprinkle with sea salt to taste and serve immediately with lemon wedges and aioli (optional).

"On a cobblestone street there is a modest little building with an awning. When I open the door, push aside the heavy curtain, and enter the warm antiques-cluttered room, I am always overcome with a rush of sheer happiness. It is always full, yet still feels like a secret."

—TAMARA JENKINS

CROQUETAS DE BACALAO

Serves 4 to 6

For the croquetas
1 pound dried bacalao (salt cod)
4 medium russet potatoes
2 cups whole milk
½ white onion, peeled
1 garlic clove
1 bay leaf
½ cup unsalted butter, cubed
1 cup all-purpose flour
1 teaspoon chopped parsley
1 teaspoon black pepper
Zest of 1 lemon
Canola oil, for frying
2 eggs
1 pound breadcrumbs
Fine sea salt, for finishing

For the Meyer lemon aioli
2 egg yolks
1 garlic clove, finely chopped
2 cups extra virgin olive oil
½ Meyer lemon
Pinch of salt

1. Rehydrate the bacalao by soaking it in a large pot of cold water for 16 to 24 hours in the refrigerator. Change the water at least three times. Once the fish is rehydrated, remove and pat dry. Using a paring knife, carefully remove the pin bones.

2. Bring a large pot of water to boil. Add the potatoes and cook until fork tender, approximately 20 minutes. Drain, let cool until tolerably hot, and peel. Coarsely grate the potatoes and set aside.

3. Combine the milk, onion, garlic, and bay leaf in a deep, heavy-bottomed pan. Bring the milk to a boil, then lower to a simmer. Add the fish and poach for 10 minutes; the fish should be opaque but still tender. Remove the fish and set aside. Strain the milk through a sieve, discard the aromatics, and set aside.

4. Make a béchamel by heating the butter in a large pan until melted but not colored. Gradually add in the flour, whisking to incorporate. Once the flour browns slightly, pour in the strained milk, stirring constantly.

5. Stir the grated potatoes into the béchamel. Flake in the bacalao using your hands. Add the chopped parsley, black pepper, and lemon zest, and stir to incorporate. Let the croquette mixture cool to room temperature or refrigerate for 20 minutes to allow the mixture to become more sculptable.

6. While the mixture cools, make the lemon aioli. Whisk together the egg yolks in a small bowl. Microplane or finely chop the garlic clove and add to the yolks. Slowly drizzle the olive oil into the yolks while whisking constantly, until the mixture attains a smooth texture. Add the juice of the Meyer lemon and a pinch of salt. Stir gently to incorporate. Set aside.

7. Form the croquettes by rolling the cod-potato mixture between your hands into 1½-inch balls. The shape is up to you; some prefer batons, others spheres. Before frying, any portion of this recipe can be frozen for future use.

8. Heat 2½ inches of canola oil in a dutch oven over medium heat until it reaches 375°F.

9. In a small bowl, beat the eggs until well incorporated; add the crumbs to another bowl. Dip the croquettes in the egg mixture, then into the breadcrumbs, making sure each croquette is well coated.

10. Working in batches, fry each croquette until golden, usually only 30 to 45 seconds per piece. Remove from the pot with a spider or slotted spoon and place on a paper towel–lined tray. Sprinkle with sea salt to taste and serve immediately with the aioli alongside.

FRIED ANCHOVIES

Fried anchovies taste best after you've been in the sea all day, after you've clambered out, towel dried, and found a seat at one of the ubiquitous patio cafés on the Mediterranean. My signal memory is from a small seaside café called Taverna La Cialoma, in Marzamemi on the southern tip of Sicily. The café is run by a wonderful woman named Lina Campisi. I went there with Danny, Roberto, Alberto, and Joaquin, my four favorite people in the world. I still remember the strips of shadow from the reed ceiling, shielding us from the afternoon sun; the salt on our skin; the sea stretching out to forever; and that type of leisurely hunger that comes from a day at the beach.

As a chef, Campisi is a master of simplicity, and her anchovies are a perfect example of this. Like pommes frites from the sea, they are more an interplay of texture than of seasoning. Crisp on the outside, tender within, they arrive in a brown paper cone. The tiny anchovies were light, airy, and golden, set off with just a lemon squeeze. Every time I eat them, I'm immediately transported back to Sicily, and that's the Proustian well to which we return when we put these on the menu at il Buco.

Serves 4

24 fresh anchovies, rinsed, gutted, and patted dry
3 pints cold sparkling water, divided
1 cup 00 flour
1 tablespoon cracked black pepper
1 tablespoon chopped fresh thyme
1 tablespoon chopped fresh oregano
1 teaspoon chili flakes
1 teaspoon salt, plus more for finishing
Canola oil, for frying
1 lemon, quartered

1. Submerge the anchovies in 2 pints sparkling water for 5 minutes.

2. Meanwhile, in a large bowl, whisk together the remaining pint of sparkling water and the flour until a batter forms. Fold in the pepper, thyme, oregano, chili flakes, and 1 teaspoon salt.

3. In a dutch oven, heat 2 inches of canola oil to 350°F.

4. Remove the anchovies from the water, pat dry, and dip each into the batter. Shake off any excess.

5. Working in batches, carefully lay the anchovies in the oil, one by one, head first. Do not allow them to touch. Fry for 30 seconds, then flip for an additional 15 seconds or so, until the anchovies are enrobed in a light golden crust.

6. Remove from the dutch oven with a spider or slotted spoon and place on a paper towel–lined tray. Sprinkle with sea salt to taste and serve immediately with lemon wedges.

CARCIOFI FRITTI

Let others have April in Paris; I'll go for March in Rome, when *carciofi romaneschi* are in season and the restaurants in the winding streets of the old Jewish ghetto proudly display towers of fresh artichokes. *Carciofi alla giudia*, also called *carciofi fritti*, are one of the greatest contributions of the *cucina ebraiche-romanesca*, the millennia-old tradition of Jewish Roman cuisine. Crisp leaves give way to a tender, nutty, and earthy center. The trick here is not only to remove any tough leaves prior to frying but also to leach out any astringency by presoaking the globes in acidulated water. Do that, and the carciofi proves itself an ingredient without equal. This is a dish about honoring not only the history of Jews in Rome but also about honoring the ingredient itself. You might never find it prepared exactly this way in Rome, but the addition of the dehydrated preserved lemon peel powder, alla Justin Smillie, is the real secret weapon.

Serves 4

16 whole baby artichokes
3 lemons, 2 halved and 1 quartered for serving
1 (7-ounce) jar preserved lemons
Olive oil or canola oil, for frying
Fine sea salt, for finishing

1. To prepare the artichokes, fill a large container with 3 quarts water. Working one artichoke at a time, peel off the tough outer leaves until you begin to see a lighter pale green color. Trim the tops of the artichokes to expose their inner leaves and trim from about ¼ inch from the bottom of the globe. Using a peeler, remove the tough dark green outer skin of the remaining stem and base. Rub cut areas of the artichokes with one of the halved lemons as you work to prevent them from browning, then add the artichokes to the water as soon as each is trimmed. Repeat with the remaining artichokes.

2. Squeeze the remaining juice from the halved lemons into the water, then add the lemon halves themselves. Allow the artichokes to marinate overnight in the refrigerator, if possible.

3. Meanwhile, preheat the oven to 200°F. Seed the preserved lemons. Spread them out in an even layer on a parchment paper–lined baking sheet. Place in the oven and let dry, approximately 2 hours. Once the lemons are dry and crisp, remove and blend in a spice grinder or blender to form a powder. Set aside.

4. When ready to cook, blanch the artichokes in boiling water for 3 to 4 minutes until the outer petals are tender. Drain and cool. Lightly crush the heart with the palm of your hand to open petals and spread them as wide as possible.

5. Heat 2½ inches of frying oil in a dutch oven to 350°F over medium-high heat. Working in batches, gently lower the artichokes into the oil and fry until golden brown and tender, 2 to 4 minutes.

6. Carefully remove the artichokes from the oil with a spider or slotted spoon and transfer them to a paper towel–lined plate. Season the artichokes with lemon powder and sea salt to taste while still hot, and serve with lemon wedges.

FRIED ZUCCHINI BLOSSOMS

From the middle of summer to the beginning of fall, the zucchini blossom makes its brief scene-stealing cameo at il Buco, and no one looks forward to them more than I do. With their crepe-paper orange petals, the flowers are the prelude to the zucchini that will follow. The flower has a delicate flavor, a whisper of zucchini, but is sturdy enough to hold up to stuffing and frying. *Fiori di zucca* are a staple in the trattorie across Calabria. There, they're stuffed with mozzarella, but since we started making our own ricotta eight years ago, I prefer to use the less gooey cheese. The anchovy cuts the ricotta's natural sweetness while the basil leaf offers an herbaceous touch to the flower's vegetal flavor. We use two flours to fry them in, a fine doppio zero (00) to provide the coat and the coarser semolina to give the flower crispness.

In one bite—or two if you're dainty—you get a burst of bright complementary flavors in nature's quenelle. But you have to work for it. Stuffing zucchini blossoms can feel like a labor of love and one that must be undertaken gently. From peeling open the petals to piping in the ricotta to rolling the flower in flour, every step must be done tenderly and with patience. But like love, all that work yields tender, tremendous results.

....

Serves 3 or 4

12 fresh zucchini blossoms
1 cup fresh ricotta cheese, strained (page 58)
6 basil leaves
6 anchovy fillets, packed in olive oil
1 pint buttermilk
2 teaspoons Espelette pepper powder, divided
1 cup 00 flour
2 cups durum flour
Canola oil, for frying
Fine sea salt, for finishing
1 lemon, quartered, for serving

1. Prepare the zucchini blossoms by gently peeling open their petals. (Gently blowing on them helps.) Using your thumb and index finger, remove the stamen.

2. Fill a piping bag with the ricotta. (If you don't have one, a tablespoon will do.) Place ½ basil leaf and ½ anchovy lengthwise in the bottom of each flower. Then pipe or spoon approximately 1 tablespoon of the ricotta into the blossom. You want them to be full but not bursting. Fold the petals to close the blossom and contain the filling.

3. In a medium-size bowl, whisk together the buttermilk and ½ teaspoon of the Espelette pepper powder.

4. In another medium-size bowl, sift together the two flours.

5. Heat 2½ inches of canola oil in a dutch oven until it reaches 350°F.

6. Gently dip the stuffed flower in the buttermilk. Shake off any excess. Then dip it in the flour mixture, gently spooning the flour over the blossom until evenly coated. If it seems as if the petals are in danger of opening, gently squeeze them back together in the palm of your hand.

7. Carefully add the blossoms to the oil and fry until golden, 3 to 4 minutes.

8. Remove the blossoms with a spider or slotted spoon and place on a paper towel–lined plate. Sprinkle with the remaining Espelette pepper powder and sea salt to taste and serve immediately with lemon wedges.

SARDINAS A LA PLANCHA

The southern coast of Spain is dotted with charming little beach cafés where you'll find sardines freshly pulled from the waters each morning. At lunch, they're served after being cooked a minute or so on a hot plancha, the sea still inside them. In New York, fresh sardines arrive on Thursdays, flown in from Portugal. As soon as we get them in, we'll add this dish to the menu. They never last long. These shimmering little fish, high in omega-3, have nothing in common with the canned variety familiar to most Americans—they're bursting with flavor and vibrancy. Even if you've never been to one of those little cafés, you're instantly transported.

At il Buco, we add a few little extras to tease out the flavors of the Mediterranean: we marinate the fish in a chermoula, a traditional marinade from North Africa, and add a bit of shaved fennel and currants to give the fish a pop of freshness. In a pinch, however, all you really need is a hot skillet or grill for the perfect snack.

Serves 4

1 teaspoon coriander seeds
¾ teaspoon cumin seeds
⅛ teaspoon Aleppo pepper or Urfa biber
¾ cup chopped fresh cilantro
1 cup plus 2 tablespoons extra virgin olive
     oil, divided
2 garlic cloves, minced
Zest of 1 lime
Fine sea salt
½ teaspoon hot paprika (optional)
8 whole sardines (1½ to 2 ounces each), scaled,
     cleaned, and patted dry
1 fennel bulb, trimmed, cored, and thinly shaved
2 tablespoons fresh red currants
Juice of ½ lemon plus 1 lemon, quartered, for serving

1. Preheat the oven to 350°F.

2. For the chermoula, place the coriander, cumin, and pepper on a small baking sheet and toast until fragrant, about 10 minutes. Let the spices cool slightly, then transfer to a spice grinder or mortar and pestle along with the cilantro. Blend into a paste. Transfer the paste to a bowl and whisk in 1 cup of olive oil, along with the garlic, lime zest, and a pinch of salt. Add the paprika if you'd like a bit of extra heat.

3. Spoon ½ cup of the prepared chermoula into a small bowl and set aside. Add the sardines to the remaining chermoula and toss to coat. Cover the bowl of sardines and place it in the refrigerator to marinate for at least 30 minutes.

4. Meanwhile, add the fennel and currants to a medium-size bowl. Drizzle with 1 tablespoon of olive oil, the lemon juice, and a pinch of salt and toss to combine.

5. Heat a large cast iron skillet over medium heat. Once the pan is hot, drizzle with the remaining tablespoon of olive oil, add the sardines, and cook, turning once, until just charred and cooked through, 1 to 1½ minutes per side. (If the pan is crowded, work in batches of 4 sardines at a time.) Alternatively, heat an outdoor grill and cook the sardines for the same amount of time. To serve, divide the fennel mixture among four plates and top each one with two sardines. Drizzle with the reserved chermoula. Sprinkle with salt to taste and serve with lemon wedges.

GAMBAS A LA SAL

Gambas a la sal, literally shrimp with salt, has been on the menu at il Buco from day one. Even before we opened, it was my favorite meal that Alberto made in the early days of our courtship. A classic tapa, it is probably the simplest to prepare but it also bursts with flavor, thanks to the inherent complexity of prawns.

With so little to add, using high-quality ingredients is even more important. We use Hawaiian blue prawns, which are large with a subtle sweetness to the meat, and our own large-grained *fiori di sale* from Trapani, in Sicily. Add a sprig of rosemary, a bit of red pepper flakes for heat, and that's it. The dish perfectly embodies our philosophy of doing the least possible to the best possible ingredients.

The magic is in the eating of it. If you didn't grow up sucking shrimp heads, you might be a little bit tentative the first time. I know I was, and some nights I see our guests at il Buco puzzling what to do with the four large prawns that come wholly intact in the order. I'll approach and show them how to peel the shrimp and implore them to slurp up the heads. "Trust me," I say, "the heads are the best part."

The inside of the prawn's head contains briny, sweet, and intense flavors, the essence of the prawn. It's the same pleasure that drives lobster lovers to eat the tomalley or crawfish connoisseurs to slowly suck out the "crawfish butter." This is the foie gras of the sea.

Serves 4

10 ounces (2 cups) coarse sea salt
16 Hawaiian blue prawns or head-on large shrimp
    (10/15 count per pound), about 20 ounces total,
    unpeeled, deveined, with heads on
4 sprigs rosemary
1 teaspoon red pepper flakes
Fine sea salt to taste
2 lemons, quartered, for serving

1. Preheat a large cast iron skillet on high. Once piping hot, sprinkle salt evenly in the skillet.

2. Working in batches if necessary, place the prawns in the skillet in a single layer, along with the sprigs of rosemary and red pepper flakes.

3. Turn the heat down to medium and cook the prawns until the shells turn opaque, 3 to 4 minutes.

4. Using tongs, gently flip the prawns and continue cooking, another 3 to 4 minutes.

5. Serve the prawns immediately, with a sprinkle of sea salt, a wedge of lemon, and a warm hand towel.

"When I first set out to write the Underground Gourmet column for New York magazine, I went to the little restaurant where Alberto Avalle was cooking on a hot plate in the back. The walls were lined with ancient radios. I fell in love and wrote my very first restaurant review about Donna and Alberto's child."

—PETER KAMINSKY

PULPO A LA GALLEGA

Galicia was Alberto's first love. He fell for the region after his self-imposed exile from Italy, and he clung to it with the passion of a drowning man. Before Alberto and I ever traveled to Italy together, we went traveling through Spain.

What sustained us and ensured that we didn't murder each other on those winding roads, in the little posadas that dot the countryside? Easy. *Pulpo a la Gallega*, eaten in the rough-and-ready *polbeirias* found throughout Galicia. Originally brought to Galicia from the coast by cattle traders, the octopus was pre-served, packed in olive oil and paprika, and eaten at fairs (thus its other name, *pulpo a feira*). Happily, now we no longer have to rely on preserved octopus. It's a simple but delicate dish: the octopus must be cooked just to tender, not chewy. The potatoes must likewise be boiled to tenderness but not to disintegration. When done right, this pairing of sea and field is divine. The proper drizzle of olive oil and a few crystals of salt are the final touch. Enjoyed with a glass of Albariño or a beautiful Manzanilla from Jerez, it salves all the day's stresses.

Serves 4

4 large Spanish octopus tentacles,
    approximately 1 pound total
1 bay leaf
½ onion
4 garlic cloves
8 medium fingerling potatoes
4 tablespoons parsley leaves, torn
3 tablespoons extra virgin olive oil
1 teaspoon smoked paprika
½ teaspoon freshly ground black pepper
Sea salt

1. To prepare the octopus, bring 1 quart of water to a boil in a large saucepan over medium heat. Add the octopus, bay leaf, onion, and garlic. Cook for 20 to 30 minutes until tender.

2. Meanwhile, bring a medium pot of salted water to a boil. Add the potatoes and cook for 25 to 30 minutes, until potatoes are tender.

3. Remove the octopus and pat dry, reserving its cooking water. Slice the tentacles into ¼-inch coins.

4. Remove the potatoes and allow to cool slightly. Slice the potatoes into coins of the same width and thickness as the octopus.

5. If necessary, reheat the reserved octopus water over medium heat. Once simmering, add the octopus and potatoes once more. Boil for about a minute to reheat. Remove both from water with a slotted spoon.

6. To serve, lay the potatoes in a single layer on a plate, top with octopus. Finish with parsley, olive oil, paprika, black pepper, and sea salt to taste.

SIZZLING BABY EELS

Angulas, or elvers, are tiny baby eels that look like shimmering translucent spaghetti. In fact, when we toss them in sizzling olive oil, rich with garlic and chili, you might mistake them for pasta aglio e olio, only with two tiny eyes and a hard-to-pin-down flavor. Other than their rarity, what makes angulas a delicacy all across the Basque Country is the hint of brininess they release into the oil as they cook and their intriguing texture when done right. They're unlike anything else: the perfect marriage of sea and land. Once a working-class tapa, angulas have become one of Spain's most prized foods.

The elvers journey from the Sargasso Sea to the Atlantic coast each year in October, when these tiny creatures fetch up to $5,500 per kilo at auction. In the States, where elvers are harvested in Maine from March to June, a kilo still runs up to $2,800. Often you'll find them at specialty stores, frozen. But if you can find them and have a little money to spend, they make a showstopping and delicious last-minute addition to the dinner table with a great Manzanilla. In the early days of il Buco, these were a prized addition to the menu, and for those in the know, worth a trip from far and wide.

Serves 4

½ cup extra virgin olive oil
2 garlic cloves, minced
½ fresh Fresno chili pepper, deseeded and sliced
1 pound fresh elvers (or frozen elvers, defrosted)
2 teaspoons chopped parsley

1. Place a 8-inch cazuela (or a small skillet) on the stovetop to preheat for 2 to 3 minutes.

2. Pour the olive oil into the cazuela, add the garlic and chili, and cook for 2 to 3 minutes, allowing the garlic to color but not burn.

3. Add the elvers to the cazuela. Allow to cook until the eels turn opaque, between 30 seconds and a minute.

4. Sprinkle with parsley and serve immediately, spooning onto individual plates at the table or passing them around tapas style.

"From its inception, il Buco has been an integral part of my culinary ritual. So many meals with students and colleagues, beautiful wines, enduring friendships, and those spectacular baby eels are still etched in my mind."

—GRAHAM NICKSON

IL VINO

_____

The first time Alberto and I descended the steep flight of stairs into the basement of 47 Bond, it was as if we'd walked straight into a secret. Rooms like this just didn't exist in New York, not even in the nineties. Long and high-ceilinged with thick stone walls that kept the temperature cool, old vaulted coal furnaces along one wall. The cavernous space was filled with canvases, tubes of oil paint, wooden easels, the equipment of a working painter.

Patricia, one of the three artists who shared the storefront, used it as her studio. Works in progress—large, circular paintings inspired by crop circles—were scattered about. She had built a wall across the belly of the room, but even that couldn't banish the genius loci. The stone walls seemed older than Manhattan; even the floor seemed primordial. It felt like an ancient crypt or a sacristy kept from the public's view. Alberto and I were already in love with the building, but this sealed the deal. We thought, at the same time and immediately, that the space would make an amazing wine cellar one day. Wine needs to be kept cool, quiet,

and unperturbed. It didn't get more unperturbed than this. Nearly two hundred years ago, Edgar Allan Poe had supposedly passed many a night around here. In the mid-1800s Bond Street was part of a notorious red-light district filled with prostitution and opium dens. It was reputed Poe drowned the sorrows of his wife's illness in the cellar there, likely with absinthe and perhaps with an occasional opium hit, shared with a "lady friend" who lived in the building. It must have been cozy. Judging from the old masonry line, the ceiling in those days was a good four feet lower than it is today. Rumor has it that it was in this basement that

LEFT: Il Buco wine cellar

Poe conceived his short tale of revenge, "The Cask of Amontillado," about a man burying his nemesis in the walls of a wine cellar. In fact, in the mid-1940s, New York University sent in an excavation crew to dig in the caves to determine if there were in fact any remains. Nothing was discovered.

Initially, the cellar served as a storage space for our new antiques store, so we left it mostly as is. But from the moment we got our wine and beer license, dated July 18, 1994 (Alberto's fortieth birthday), we began plotting to create that wine cellar. Alberto and I gathered a handful of distributors, determined to make a small boutique list in our little wine/tapas bar. We would serve a small menu of inspired tapas accompanied by a wine list of little-known producers respecting terroir. We were guided by the predilections of Alberto, though we eventually brought in the expertise of our dear client, Jonathan Nossiter, a kindred spirit in zest for life and purist approach to all things wine. Additionally, we shared a love of film. I'll never forget the first day we met to discuss our collaboration. Jonathan invited us to his little apartment in Nolita. He served a delicious pasta lunch with a bottle of Marqués de Murietta Rioja Blanco. This golden-yellow, slightly oxidized wine with nutty tones and rich acidity initiated our collaboration.

Under Jonathan's guidance, Alberto and I began to fill the room with bottles of the Spanish, Italian, and American wines Alberto loved so much. There was an unusual selection of Mediterranean wines, including old-style Riojas, like Rioja Alta, Muga, and Lopéz de Heredia, and the iconic Château Musar of Lebanon. But our list also included manzanillas, olorosos, and amontillados from Andalucía and an ample number of Madeiras and ports. We went to work to turn the space into a proper cellar. Borrowing a system we saw in a wine bar in Spain, and with the help of our old friend Jimmy Galuppo of Etna Tool & Die across Bond Street, we installed iron castings along the ceiling, in which the bottles could rest and made iron gates to close the wine inside the three old coal beds along the

back right wall of the space. From Warren Muller, one of the original artists in the space, we bought one of his curlicue chandeliers, which filled the cellar walls with a lovely romantic light, and schlepped a table we had found in Pennsylvania down the steep flight. Because we didn't have a Certificate of Occupancy, we couldn't technically host anyone down there, but occasionally our regulars would surreptitiously find their way downstairs to smoke cigarettes and drink glasses of rare auction wines well into the night.

At the end of the day, however, we were a small tapas bar, mostly an antique store, with an idiosyncratic wine program with modest ambition. Jonathan's life turned to film, beginning with *Sunday* and then to the documentary *Mondovino* and books such as *Liquid Memory: Why Wine Matters*. His travels took him farther and farther away, but the friendship has lasted these twenty-five years. How did we go from then to now, when the cellar is overflowing with some of the world's best wines and our list hovers around eight hundred offerings? Simple: a man named Roberto Paris.

I'll never forget the day in 1997 when a tall Italian man with scraggly dreadlock-like hair approached me outside on the terrace. Our first review in *New York* magazine had recently come out. He asked me if he could speak with the owner. "You are," I replied, "I'm the owner."

"Isn't there also an Italian owner?" he inquired.

"Yes," I said, "that's my partner, Alberto. I'll run upstairs and get him."

The surprise on Alberto's face when he stepped onto the patio was epic. He and Roberto had grown up together in Foligno. As mentioned before, Alberto had had a rift with his family, and no one knew where he had landed. Roberto had been living with his brother in Westchester and came across the article. That first reunion lasted many hours but is now nearly twenty-three years strong. Alberto insisted that Roberto drop his day job and come and work with us at il Buco. He was persuasive. A few months later

RIGHT: Roberto Paris, wine director

46

Roberto started, and he never left. Over the years he had many roles and wore many hats in the restaurant, but his most important—aside from always being my right hand, best friend, and the godfather of my son, Joaquin—was being an extraordinary wine director and spirit guide of the restaurant.

When Roberto Paris was a boy growing up in a small village across the valley from Foligno called Colle San Lorenzo in the 1950s, he knew he didn't fit into the world into which he was born. His father, Edmondo, was a poor mason and a farmer who had spent World War II as an English prisoner of war held in Tasmania. (His mother, Luisa, meanwhile endured the ravages of wartime alone, raising Roberto's older siblings.) Had the war not taken him around the world, Edmondo never would have left. Luisa never did. For the inhabitants of San Lorenzo, the scope of their lives was the scope of their eyes, rolling hills, olive groves, crumbling walls. Even in the 1950s, electricity was intermittent. Many houses had no running water. There was one television, which the village priest owned. For the first decade of his life, Roberto never left the town either.

With a much older brother and sister, and busy parents, Roberto was often left to his own devices. But he was an insatiable reader, mostly self-taught, and an inveterate dreamer. He devoured any book he could get his hands on. As the only bibliophile in his family, this chubby little boy with Pontormo eyes was a mystery to those closest to him. And as the world opened up to him from his small room in the volumes he read, he came to realize how different he was from the rest of the people in his village. It wasn't until he read Hans Christian Andersen's "The Ugly Duckling" that he truly found himself. Or rather, he found that he could *be* himself, regardless of where he was from or where an accident of fate had deposited him.

When Roberto was ten or eleven, the local priest approached Roberto's parents and told them that their son, who had so lovely a voice he was picked to sing the Ave Maria at the local church, had a calling to join the priesthood. They agreed—his mother more than

his father, an old Fascist who distrusted the church—and, from this little town, Roberto would travel across the valley to Foligno to attend a seminary school for young boys. The most salient detail here isn't that, as the prelate soon discovered, he was an incorrigible troublemaker, or that, in fact, he didn't believe in God—though he loved the solemn ceremony of Mass—but that the church had a library filled with both secular and religious texts. The calling that Roberto soon discovered that he had wasn't toward the divine, but toward adventure. Filling hours reading James Fenimore Cooper, Jules Verne, the Italian swashbuckling novelist Emilio Salgari, and a massive multivolume encyclopedia called *I Treccani* that contained, he thought at the time, the knowledge of the world, Roberto knew he had to explore the world, he had to get out of Foligno. And get out he did.

By the time he walked into Bond Street, Roberto was forty-two years old. He had lived an entire life. He had been a student in Rome and spent years traveling the world, through Italy, France, Germany, India, before returning to Foligno. There he opened an iconic enoteca, il Bacco Felice, with his friend Salvatore Denaro, with whom he shared a love of wine and life. In 1994 he secured a visa that landed him in the United States just as we were opening il Buco. Most recently he had been in San Francisco, he told us, installing spotlights in galleries and museums, mostly because it afforded him the chance to be alone with art.

Once Roberto joined the il Buco family, he and Alberto began their most personal quest, to bring Sagrantino, the sacred wine of Umbria, to New York. For Alberto and Roberto, the Sagrantino grape is part of their proud wine patrimony. Originally brought to the region by monks for making sacramental wine, the thick-skinned grape flourished in the long hot summers of the region. It became intimately tied with the land and Perugians. According to legend, falconers from nearby Montefalco would use a few drops to salve the wounds inflicted by the sharp talons of their charges. (A few glasses, I'm sure, further dulled the pain.) High

CLOCKWISE FROM TOP LEFT: Arnaldo Caprai vineyards, Montefalco, Italy; Roberto and Donna, Arnaldo Caprai Vineyards; Alberto, Donna, Salvatore, Roberto, Antonello, Neri, Clelia; Alberto and Salvatore Denaro; Roberto and Marco Caprai; wine barrels, Cantina Arnaldo Caprai FOLLOWING: Post luncheon wineglasses, Alain Passard's farm

in tannins and yet still quite elegant, Sagrantino has always had the potential to make great wine. But for years, decades, centuries, Sagrantino had been overlooked as a serious grape. It was thought suitable only for *passito*, or sweet, wines, or used as a wingman in Sangiovese blends. Even in Montefalco itself, the region in which Foligno and Colle San Lorenzo both sit, the grape's potential had never been realized.

However, in the 1971, a man named Arnaldo Caprai, a textile entrepreneur turned winemaker, bought twelve and a half acres of land in Montefalco with the idea of rescuing Sagrantino from the hinterlands of wine. For fifteen years, Arnaldo experimented with the Sagrantino, but it wasn't until his son, Marco, took over in 1988 that the development of Sagrantino began in earnest. Together with the University of Milan, Marco began to selectively breed the rootstock, quadrant by quadrant, selecting clones that distilled and showcased the natural qualities of the grape. For the first time, Sagrantino was being treated with the respect it deserved. The wines rewarded the care. With Marco's monomaniacal attention, the wines rose to the level of DOCG, the highest of Italy's denominations. Now, by law, Sagrantino must be aged thirty-seven months, with twelve of those months in new oak barrels.

In New York, even in 1996, Sagrantino was still an unheard-of varietal, difficult to find and known only to people—like Alberto and Roberto—who carried a bit of Montefalco with them. Alberto had been trying to find it since day one with no luck, and I know that it galled him to have his grape unavailable. Our first experience of the grape was in unmarked bottles of wine Alberto would bring back in his suitcase, like contraband, made by the locals in Montefalco. It was the housemade wine his father drank for years. It was full bodied, full fruit, and luscious with the strong tannic undertone; I fell in love with it too. I relished its arrival but kept our few precious bottles for personal use.

For Roberto, who had grown up reading the work of the Italian anarchist Luigi Veronelli, a man who relentlessly fought for local-ness, the valorization of Sagrantino went beyond pride, beyond wine, and took on a moral component. He immediately understood what Alberto wanted and, with a twinkle in his eye, said, "Let me see what I can do."

The next day, he showed up at il Buco with two cases of Sagrantino. The producer was an elderly gentleman named Paolo Bea, at that time making wines next to the barnyard where he kept his livestock. This was the only Sagrantino in New York, brought by a prescient boutique importer named Neal Rosenthal. In that act of procurement, Roberto had demonstrated that he understood what we were about at il Buco and had the chops to play along. In the course of a few years, he managed to fill the list with a diverse group of Sagrantino producers, and others eventually followed suit. Adanti, Scacciadiavoli, Antonelli, Antano; the list continued to grow over time. In the end Roberto would be credited for almost singlehandedly bringing that grape to the attention and adoration of the American market.

I believe his success derived from the fact that although he had worked in wine for years, Roberto wasn't a wine guy. He was a seeker of stories. As it happened in his life, the avenue through which he told his stories was a wine list and that has been great for us and everyone who walks into il Buco. Distributors across the city love working with him for this reason and more. His reputation grew steadily over time with a respect that few received in the industry, in spite of his playful title of curmudgeon. Some of the relationships run long and deep and led to lasting friendships with distributors who have become part of the fabric of il Buco, like Violante Lepore of Selected Estates. Friends such as Livio Panebianco and Ned Benedict, who, sadly, are no longer with us, we honor in this book.

In building the list, Roberto continually sought likeminded travelers. He built our portfolio less around the wines themselves and more around the people behind them. This relationship-focused philosophy defines the heart of our wine program. We work

CLOCKWISE FROM TOP LEFT: Roberto Paris at Domaine du Gros Chesnay; cellar, Maison Billecart-Salmon, Mareuil-sur-Ay, France; Tom Byrnes at Domaine du Gros Chesnay; wine tasting il Buco cellar; country road, Loire Valley, France; Alain Passard kitchen; sunflower field, Roncofreddo, Italy

mostly with small family producers who respect the terroir from which their wines originate, allowing the peculiarities of the soils and the regions from which they come to emerge. These are the "ugly ducklings" that resonated so strongly with him as a boy.

Roberto and I have taken many journeys together in search of those kindred spirits. These journeys took us to San Gimignano, where Elisabetta Fagiuoli, a self-taught eighty-eight-year-old nonna, has done for Vernaccia what Marco Caprai did for Sagrantino; to the extreme corner of northern Patagonia, where Piero Incisa—the scion of the iconic Sassicaia wine family—exiled himself in an abandoned vineyard to test his mettle. The wine he makes there at Bodega Chacra is 100 percent old vine pinot noir made biodynamically.

We traveled through Spain, from Rioja to Penedès, Rias Baixas and the Duero, with André Tamers, a renegade Spanish wine importer, to taste the wines of Sastre, Do Ferreiro, and Emilio Rojo, some of our all-time favorite producers. Most recently we've collaborated with Pepe Raventos in bringing his glorious vintages of sparkling and still wines from the Penedès to our newest outpost in Ibiza, across the sea from his Catalan winery.

We've taken many visits to California with Rob and Maria Sinskey, walking through their biodynamic vineyard in the Napa Valley. Their beautiful wines, and those of André, are brought to us in New York City by our friend and distributor Tom Byrnes. The connections are endless. Last year in celebration of our shared twenty-fifth anniversaries we met Tom and a host of those mutual friends for a lunch at the farm of Alain Passard and toasted our shared passion with the wines of Billecart-Salmon.

At this point, Roberto is family. He and Joaquin have a relationship that runs deeper than I can fathom. Roberto has come to know my palate like no one else. I can fondly remember all the family holidays when he racked his brain to find just the right wine to please my dad, and how tickled he was when my dad chose Sagrantino.

Last summer, we traveled back to Foligno. It was the first time Roberto had been back to Umbria in five years, the first time he had returned to his village since an earthquake had rendered his family home uninhabitable in 2016. It was nevertheless joyous. We went to visit our friend Marco Caprai for a picnic at the winery, which began with fresh ripe figs drizzled with the best Moraiolo olive oil. (Again, those wonderful figs!) Marco drove us through the neatly planted vineyard. From the early muddied rootstocks, now each row of vines has its own distinct character, accomplished by decades of hard work. Twenty-five years after Roberto walked into il Buco, the fate of Sagrantino looked drastically different. Marco himself has flourished, his destiny tied to this grape, his father Arnaldo's legacy firmly in his hands.

Watching Roberto walk with Joaquin through the brilliant leaves of the vineyard, his village on the opposite hillside, I saw him, for the first time in a long time, at home. This experience is in many ways what Roberto has created at il Buco. Descending into the wine cellar and drinking one of the many bottles lining those caves is like taking a journey to any number of places around the world and somehow managing to feel more at home than you ever have before.

"I met Roberto the first night in my apartment on Bond Street when the rumbling of the 6 train kept me awake. He brought me a wine from Puglia and four perfectly seared pieces of tuna dressed with the most extraordinary olive oil. For more than 20 years I've been going to il Buco for something special, to remind me that the rumble of the 6 train isn't a rumble at all but the distant roll and wash of the Mediterranean."

—LIEV SCHREIBER

LEFT: Roberto and Joaquin, Caprai Vineyards

HOUSEMADE RICOTTA & SUGAR SNAPS

I fell in love with ricotta on my first visit to Italy, and it has been a staple for me ever since. My early breakfasts in Italy began with fresh ricotta from the local alimentari over a slice of toasted bread with a drizzle of local honey. Like butter, there's both magic and ease in making ricotta at home. And nothing can beat a dollop of the rich, creamy, freshly made cheese. In this simple preparation, which takes just a few minutes of active time to make, that creaminess is given a boost by the sweet, crunchy sugar snaps tossed in bright lemon juice. It's one of those snacks that's so delicious, it's hard to believe it is so easy to prepare.

Serves 4

For the ricotta (this yields approximately 4 cups in total)
2 quarts whole milk
1 cup heavy cream
½ teaspoon sea salt, plus additional for finishing
3 tablespoons fresh lemon juice

For the salad
1 pound fresh sugar snap peas, trimmed, with some sliced in half lengthwise
2 tablespoons extra virgin olive oil, divided
1 teaspoon lemon juice
1 tablespoon torn fresh mint

1. To make the ricotta, heat the milk and cream in a heavy-bottomed saucepan over medium heat until temperature reaches 110°F, for approximately 6 minutes. Be sure not to allow dairy to boil.

2. Remove the pan from the heat, stir in the salt and lemon juice, and let it stand at least an hour until the mixture curdles.

3. Line a sieve with cheesecloth and place over a large bowl. Carefully pour the mixture into the sieve. Bundle up the cheesecloth with the curds inside and squeeze to remove as much liquid as possible. The more liquid you remove, the denser the cheese will be. Allow to continue to drain overnight in the refrigerator to remove excess liquid.

4. To make the salad, place sugar snaps in a medium-size bowl. Toss with 1 tablespoon olive oil and the lemon juice. Let marinate 20 to 30 minutes to tenderize the snap peas.

5. Spoon ⅔ cup of ricotta into 4 small bowls. (Reserve remaining ricotta for another use.) Top each with the sugar snap peas, drizzle with the remaining olive oil, sprinkle with salt, and garnish with mint.

RADISHES IN BAGNA CAUDA

Radishes and anchovies are a classic flavor combination, and you'll find this dish all across Northern Italy. I think it was Jody Williams who brought this to us at il Buco. We've had it on the menu since. Traditionally, one dips the radishes in a ramekin of warm *bagna cauda*, but here we simply drizzle the sauce over the radishes and toss. Either way, the bagna cauda, ennobled by olive oil and roasted garlic, really makes the radishes pop, and vice versa. Here we call for breakfast and easter radishes, but any number of the multitude of varieties of radish create a visual spectacle at the table.

Serves 4

1 teaspoon salted capers
12 anchovy fillets, packed in olive oil
1 garlic clove
1 tablespoon red wine vinegar
½ cup extra virgin olive oil
Zest and juice of 1 lemon, divided
⅛ teaspoon chili flakes (optional)
24 breakfast and easter radishes
    (approximately one bunch total)

1. Soak the capers in cold water for 30 minutes to desalinate. Drain, dry, and set aside.

2. Grind the anchovies, capers, and garlic together with a mortar and pestle, until they reach a paste-like texture. Put the paste into a bowl. Drizzle in the vinegar and ¼ cup of the olive oil to thin out the paste. Add the lemon zest, lemon juice, and chili flakes and stir to incorporate.

3. Meanwhile, cut the breakfast radishes in half and the easter radishes in quarters. Place the radishes in a bowl of cold water with a few ice cubes to retain crispness.

4. To finish the bagna cauda, heat the remaining ¼ cup olive oil in a cast iron skillet over medium heat until shimmering. Add the bagna cauda paste, constantly stirring until the mixture turns light brown, about 5 minutes.

5. Drain the radishes and place on a platter. Pour the bagna cauda mixture into a separate dish or ramekin and serve next to the radishes for dipping. Alternatively, pour the mixture over the radishes in a bowl and serve.

BEEF TARTARE WITH SUNCHOKES

Ignacio Mattos (Nacho), our chef, was mad about this dish when he arrived from Uruguay, and I can see why. Nacho is an expert at textural interplay, and this preparation showcases his mastery: the crunch of the sunchoke chips, the texture of the beef, the silken emulsification of the vinegar and olive oil. It's enough to make someone like me, who doesn't gravitate toward raw meat on the menu, into a fan. And of course there's the il Buco twist. Though traditional beef tartare relies on Worcestershire sauce, here we use *colatura*, a deliciously briny but less fishy condiment made from the slow pressing of Sicilian anchovies. The liquid is eventually strained and bottled and contains the highest nutrients and omega-3s. We get ours directly from Baldo Scalia, our favorite anchovy producer in Sciacca, Sicily.

Serves 4

¾ pound sirloin

Neutral oil, such as grapeseed or canola, for frying

4 large sunchokes, peeled and sliced paper-thin on a mandoline (about 1½ cups sliced)

1 large shallot, minced (about ½ cup)

2 tablespoons extra virgin olive oil, plus more for drizzling

1 tablespoon finely minced chives

1 tablespoon colatura

1 tablespoon red wine vinegar

½ teaspoon fine sea salt, plus more for finishing

⅛ teaspoon freshly ground black pepper

4 quail or chicken egg yolks

Special equipment needed: mandoline

1. Place the sirloin in the freezer until semi-frozen, 30 minutes to 1 hour, depending on thickness. Remove, slice lengthwise into ⅛-inch-thick sheets, then ⅛-inch strips, then into ⅛-inch dice. Return the minced steak to the refrigerator.

2. Add 3 inches of the frying oil to a dutch oven and heat over medium high until it reads 350°F. Gently add the sunchokes and fry until golden, approximately 4 minutes. Once they are done, use a slotted spoon to transfer the crisps to a paper towel to drain.

3. In a large nonreactive bowl, mix the meat, shallot, 2 tablespoons olive oil, chives, colatura, vinegar, ½ teaspoon sea salt, and pepper together with a wooden spoon until the olive oil emulsifies and the mass holds its shape.

4. To serve, equally divide the tartare among four plates and flatten each portion into a disc or use a 3-inch ring mold. Top each one with a raw egg yolk, drizzle with additional olive oil, sprinkle with sea salt, and garnish with sunchoke chips.

"Pushing through the heavy and— somehow for no explainable reason—awkward door always feels like the appropriate way to transition from outside to inside il Buco. Once you're in you're in."

—SAM ROCKWELL

FARM EGG WITH BLACK TRUFFLES

Umbria produces the most black truffles in Italy, thanks to the clay-limestone soil and abundant forests, and Umbrian families keep their hidden truffle spots closely held secrets. During black truffle season, which lasts from October to November, you're likely to see cars ditched by the side of the road while their inhabitants are off in the forest hunting for these precious flavorful mushrooms. No wonder. Aside from being costly, black truffles burst with flavor and, perhaps even more so, a wonderfully woodsy, nutty, earthy aroma. In this recipe, both the egg and the polenta serve to support and showcase the truffles' flavor. The creamy polenta and a perfectly poached egg from Westwind Orchard or Flying Pigs Farm, together with the delicately shaved truffles, form a wonderfully comforting and luxurious combination that brings me immediately back to Umbria.

Serves 8

1 pint whole milk
1 pint Anson Mills yellow polenta
Extra virgin olive oil
8 large eggs
2 tablespoons finely grated Parmigiano-Reggiano
2 tablespoons unsalted butter
½ teaspoon sea salt, plus more for finishing
1 medium Umbrian black truffle (or Perigord truffle, or Australian black truffle in summer)

Special equipment needed: truffle shaver or mandoline

1. Add the whole milk and two pints of water to a large saucepan. Bring to a simmer over medium heat, uncovered. Slowly add the polenta, stirring with a wooden spoon or whisk to prevent lumps. Cook over low heat until the grains have plumped and softened and the mixture has thickened, about 45 minutes, stirring often so the polenta does not stick to the bottom of the pan.

2. For a nifty egg-poaching trick, line the inside of a ramekin with a piece of plastic wrap, draping it over the sides. Rub the inside of the plastic with oil. Crack an egg gently into the middle of the ramekin, then bring together the four corners of the plastic and begin to twist ¼ inch above the egg, removing any excess air, and continue twisting until you have enough space to tie it off, placing the knot as close to egg as possible. Repeat with each egg.

3. Bring a pot of water to boil. Carefully lower four wrapped eggs into the water and poach until the whites are just set and the yolks are still runny, about 4 to 5 minutes. Remove the eggs with a slotted spoon and set aside. Repeat with the remaining eggs.

4. Once the polenta is ready—it should melt in your mouth—remove from the heat and stir in the Parmigiano-Reggiano cheese, butter, and salt.

5. To plate, divide the polenta among eight bowls. Carefully remove the eggs from their plastic and place them on top of the polenta. Drizzle lightly with olive oil and season with a pinch of sea salt.

6. Using a truffle shaver, shave a few slices of black truffle over each bowl. Serve immediately.

HUEVOS A LO POBRE

My dad grew up in Brooklyn eating bagels and lox, and eggs and smoked salmon. But this dish, brought to il Buco by Ignacio Mattos, was by far his favorite breakfast. The term *a lo pobre* ("poor man's") is used widely in Peruvian and Chilean cuisine. It refers to a protein—sometimes *bistec* or *lomo*—served with fried eggs, often fried onions, and some carbohydrate, usually French fries. But when Nacho arrived at il Buco, he removed the meat and brought the dish an upgrade that included the addition of shaved bottarga—air-cured grey mullet roe—and turned the fried onions into a salad of capers, parsley, and sliced raw onions, which added a little kick. Although my dad ate this at breakfast, we serve it for lunch and dinner at the restaurant too. There's something that feels decadent about eating a fried egg at night, especially topped with bottarga.

Serves 2

½ bunch parsley, roughly chopped
¼ red onion, thinly sliced
2 teaspoons salted capers, rinsed and drained
2 tablespoons extra virgin olive oil, divided,
  plus more to taste
Juice of ½ lemon
¼ teaspoon fine sea salt, plus additional to taste
2 (½-inch) slices filone or country bread
1 garlic clove, peeled
4 large eggs
4 ounces bottarga di muggine, finely grated
Freshly ground black pepper to taste

1. Preheat the oven to 350°F.

2. Toss the parsley, onion, capers, 1 teaspoon olive oil, lemon juice, and sea salt together in a bowl. Set aside.

3. Place the bread on a baking sheet and toast in the oven until it develops a nice crust. Rub the top of the bread with the garlic clove and drizzle with 2 teaspoons of olive oil.

4. In a cast iron pan, heat the remaining tablespoon of oil over medium heat until shimmering.

5. Carefully break the eggs into the pan, making sure the yolks stay whole.

6. After a minute or so, place the pan in the oven for 45 seconds until the whites are set but the yolks are still soft. To serve, divide the eggs onto two plates with a spoonful of the parsley salad and toasted bread. Shave the bottarga over the top of the eggs. Sprinkle with salt and pepper to taste.

"I have a fond memory of shaking hands with the wonderful Francis Alÿs when he decided midway through dinner to accept my offer to join the gallery. It was a celebration of food, art, and life."

—DAVID ZWIRNER

FRIED RABBIT WITH ROSEMARY

Jody Williams, our second chef after Thierry, brought this dish with her back from her time working in Reggio-Emilia. In some ways it's the embodiment of her food: tasty, delicious, and home-cooked. To be honest, rabbit was a hard sell at first—sometimes the worst part of eating rabbit is that you're eating rabbit—but Alberto fell in love with the preparation of it. It reminded him of how he ate growing up in Foligno: "It's a taste from my home," he'd enthuse. Jody's secret was to allow enough excess flour to remain in the dredging so that there were all these wonderful little crispy bits that accompanied the succulent pieces of rabbit, which were in perfect crunchy bite-size pieces.

Serves 4

1 fryer rabbit, approximately 3 pounds, boned out
1 quart buttermilk
2 garlic cloves, peeled
½ teaspoon crushed peperoncino
4 sprigs rosemary, plus 1 sprig, leaves chopped
2 teaspoons fine sea salt, divided, plus more
    for finishing
Canola oil, for frying
2 cups all-purpose flour
1 cup semolina flour
½ teaspoon freshly ground black pepper

1. Starting with the loins, cut each in half crosswise. For the thighs, place each one skin side down and cut each thigh into 3 to 5 even pieces. Leave front legs whole.

2. Add the buttermilk, garlic, peperoncino, chopped rosemary, and 1 teaspoon fine sea salt to a blender and blend until smooth. Pour the marinade into a large bowl. Add the rabbit, toss until well coated, and cover tightly with plastic wrap. Transfer to the refrigerator and marinate for 8 hours or overnight.

3. About 1 hour before you are ready to fry, remove the rabbit from the refrigerator and let it come to room temperature.

4. Heat the oven to 200°F. Pour 3 inches of the neutral oil into a large dutch oven and place over medium-high heat until it reaches 350°F.

5. As the oil heats, whisk together the flours and 1 teaspoon salt and the pepper and spread in a shallow bowl. Remove the rabbit pieces from the marinade, shaking off any excess liquid. Dredge each piece in the flour mixture until thickly coated (don't worry about shaking off excess flour; these will become delicious crispy bits later on).

6. Carefully lower 2 or 3 pieces of rabbit into the hot oil. Fry until crispy and golden on all sides and the internal temperature is 160°F, approximately 8 minutes, adding the remaining sprigs of rosemary to the oil for the last minute. Transfer the finished rabbit and rosemary pieces to a paper towel–lined baking sheet and transfer to the oven to keep warm. Continue frying in batches until all the rabbit has been used, making sure to maintain the oil at a steady 350°F.

7. Serve the rabbit immediately with fried rosemary sprigs and a sprinkle of sea salt.

BOTIFARRA WITH PEACHES

Il Buco chef Roger Martinez had a storied career at some of Spain's best restaurants. But it wasn't his time with Ferran and Albert Adria, the Roca brothers, or his years with Carles Abellán at La Barra, or even his experience with David Bouley here in New York that enticed me. It was his ability to bring the unique flavors of Spain to il Buco with his own touch. After all, if Italy is the mother country from which the il Buco spirit derives, the Iberian peninsula has always been the doting aunt.

Botifarra is a unique Catalonian sausage, unlike most other sausages, that is boiled then grilled. Roger makes his with Iberico pork shoulder and a little bit of belly. The meats get a nice char on the grill, as do the caramelized grilled peaches, which are a perfect counterpoint to the gamey pork.

Serves 4 to 6

2 pounds skinless pork shoulder (preferably Iberico), cut into 1-inch pieces
2 ounces pork belly
4 teaspoons coarse sea salt
¾ teaspoon pink curing salt
3 feet medium-size natural casing, soaked in 2 changes of lukewarm water for a total of 2 hours
1 tablespoon olive oil, plus more for dressing
4 peaches, halved and pitted
Leaves from 1 bunch mustard greens
Sea salt and freshly ground black pepper

Special equipment needed: stand mixer with meat grinder and sausage stuffer attachment

1. In a large bowl, mix the pork shoulder, belly, coarse salt, and curing salt together. Place the mixture in the freezer just until meat reaches 32°F. Using a stand mixer with a meat grinder attachment, grind the meat through a coarse die (¼-inch plate or #5) into a chilled bowl. Pass half of the meat through the grinder again. Mix together and refrigerate until cold.

2. Rinse the casing well with cold water and feed onto a large tube of the sausage stuffer attachment on a stand mixer. Tie a knot at the end of the casing and pierce it gently with the tip of a toothpick. Pass the meat from the stuffer into the casing, making sure the meat is densely packed. Once you have used all the meat, twist the sausages into 4-inch lengths. Tie off the casing after the last sausage. Trim excess casing. Using a toothpick, prick the sausage a few times per link.

3. To prepare, bring a large pot of salted water to boil. Lower the heat to a low simmer, gently add the sausages, and poach for 10 minutes. Meanwhile, prepare an ice bath by filling a medium bowl with ice and cold water. Plunge the sausages into the ice bath to arrest cooking.

4. Heat a cast iron skillet over high heat with 1 tablespoon olive oil. Remove the sausages from the ice bath and gently pat dry. Add to the skillet and sear on all sides, turning as needed, until browned all over, approximately 5 minutes. Transfer the sausages to a plate and keep warm.

5. Add the peaches to the skillet, cut side down. Sear until browned, about five minutes. Dress the mustard greens lightly with oil and season with salt and pepper.

6. To serve, arrange the sausages and peaches, divided among four plates, garnish with greens, and season with sea salt to taste.

LAMB RIBS WITH ROMESCO

The first time I had this lamb at il Buco, I was blown away. When done low and slow, the meat gets beautifully caramelized, sealing in the rendered fat which, along with the brine, gives the meat so much of its flavor. The spice-rich rub, meanwhile, removes some of the "lambiness," while the spicy and sweet romesco gives the fatty lamb the acidic counterpart it needs. The result is a compulsively eatable dish that's just as nice in the fall and winter as it is in the summer and spring.

....

Serves 4

2 whole racks of lamb ribs, fat trimmed

For the brine
2 cups kosher salt
½ white onion
4 garlic cloves
2 bay leaves
1 sprig rosemary
1 sprig thyme
6 dried allspice berries
Peel of 1 lime

For the harissa rub
1 cup olive oil
1¾ pounds diced tomato (approximately 2 cups)
4 garlic cloves, grated
2 tablespoons paprika
1 tablespoon ground coriander seed
1 tablespoon ground cumin
1 tablespoon Aleppo pepper
1 tablespoon sumac
3 saffron threads (optional)
½ teaspoon sea salt

For the romesco sauce
1 cup white bread, interior only
1 cup canned piquillo peppers, drained
½ cup Marcona almonds, toasted
½ cup hazelnuts, toasted and skins rubbed off
½ cup olive oil
2 tablespoons red wine or sherry vinegar
1 garlic clove

1 teaspoon smoked paprika
1 teaspoon dried chili flakes
½ teaspoon sea salt, plus more for finishing

1. To prepare the brine, combine all the ingredients with 4 quarts of water in a large pot and bring to a boil, uncovered. Once a boil has been reached, turn off the heat and let cool. Once cool, add the ribs. Cover and refrigerate for 16 to 24 hours.

2. To make the harissa rub, heat the olive oil in a large skillet over medium heat, then add the remaining harissa ingredients. Bring to a simmer and cook for 15 minutes. Let cool and then blend into a paste in a food processor or blender.

3. After the required time, remove the ribs from the brine and pat dry. Using your hands, rub the harissa in an even coat all over the ribs. Let sit for at least 30 minutes or overnight in the refrigerator.

4. To cook the ribs, preheat the oven to 275°F. Place the ribs on a baking rack set on a baking sheet and cook for approximately 3 hours or until tender. Then increase the temperature to 375°F and let cook for another 45 minutes. Remove from oven and let rest for 15 minutes, then cut into individual ribs.

5. To make the romesco, blend together all ingredients in a food processor or blender for 20 to 60 seconds.

6. Serve two to three ribs per person, seasoned with salt, on a spoonful of romesco.

ROASTED QUAIL WITH ZA'ATAR

When Sara Jenkins arrived at il Buco in 2000, she brought with her a quiver of deeply flavorful but totally approachable recipes, forged from a lifetime of traveling the Mediterranean. Sara's father, Loren, was a foreign correspondent. Her mother, Nancy Harmon Jenkins, a legendary food writer. Sara had grown up hopscotching from cuisine to cuisine, with a large part of her childhood spent in Lebanon and later in Tuscany where the family had a country home. By the time she came to our kitchen, Sara had spent a good deal of time cooking in Florence and Tuscan wine country.

I have fond memories of a trip to northern Spain and Tuscany with Sara and Roberto—an eating frenzy—that ended with a home-cooked meal at Sara's lovely Tuscan home.

This recipe was, and is, by far one of my favorites of her preparations. It embodies what makes Sara Sara, a seemingly effortless dish that modestly cloaks immense talent. In it, crispy quail, humming with za'atar spice, is accompanied by Umbrian lentils, straight from the plateau of Casteluccio, famous for their ability to hold their texture after cooking.

Serves 4

4 quail, semiboneless
7 tablespoons extra virgin olive oil, divided,
    plus additional for finishing
1 tablespoon sea salt, divided,
    plus additional for finishing
2 tablespoons za'atar spice
Freshly ground black pepper
1 medium white onion, sliced
1 leek, trimmed, washed, and thinly sliced
2 garlic cloves, chopped
1 sprig sage leaves
2 cups Umbrian lentils
2 cups dry white wine
2 teaspoons torn parsley for garnish

1. Rinse the quail and pat dry. Rub with 2 tablespoons of the olive oil and 1 teaspoon of sea salt, then sprinkle with za'atar spice and pepper. Let sit uncovered in the refrigerator from 45 minutes to overnight.

2. To prepare the lentils, heat 2 tablespoons of olive oil in a large skillet over medium heat until shimmering. Add the onion, leek, garlic, sage, and 1 teaspoon of salt, cooking over low heat until the onion turns translucent, the leek tender, and the garlic gold, approximately 5 to 7 minutes.

3. Add the lentils, wine, and 2½ cups water, stirring gently. Bring to a boil then simmer uncovered and cook until tender, approximately 15 to 20 minutes.

4. Meanwhile, remove the quail from the refrigerator and allow to come to room temperature. Heat 3 tablespoons of the olive oil over medium-high heat until shimmering in a cast iron skillet. Add the quail, breast side down, and cook until golden, about 7 minutes. Then flip and cook for another 5 minutes.

5. To serve, equally divide the lentils among four plates and top each with a quail and a sprinkle of parsley. Season with sea salt and a drizzle of olive oil.

"Over these past 20 plus years, il Buco has provided the dining table at which to think, to interact, to debate, to love, and to eat so very well!"
—ROBERT ENSERRO

BLACK RICE WITH SAUSAGE & SHRIMP

I've always loved the toothsome flavorful *riso nero* of Venice. With a lovely nuttiness and slightly sweet finish, the rice works just as well in a summer salad as it does in a risotto. But I think it's at its best when paired with strong flavors, flavors that would overpower a more delicate rice. Garrison Price, our chef at il Buco Alimentari from 2017 to 2019, first came up with this dish. What I love about it is how the sea flavor of the shrimp, the spice of the Calabrian sausage, and the creaminess of the egg yolk play with the nuttiness of the rice. Something about the combination of these ingredients with the addition of leeks lends an Asian timbre to this dish, but I assure you it's fully Mediterranean. It's not something I ever would have thought of, but as soon as we put it on the menu, it became a best seller. And it still is.

Serves 4

4 large egg yolks
1½ tablespoons fine sea salt, plus additional to taste
1 cup plus 1 tablespoon olive oil, divided
1 medium leek, cleaned
1½ cups Venetian black rice
¼ pound fennel sausage (for homemade, see page 78)
½ pound (16/20 count per pound) raw shrimp, peeled, deveined, and diced
2 garlic cloves, minced
Freshly ground black pepper
2 tablespoons tomato puree
1 teaspoon chopped Calabrian chili (about 1 chili)
1 tablespoon minced fresh parsley leaves
1 tablespoon minced chives

1. Cure the egg yolks: In a medium bowl, dissolve salt into 1 quart of water. Gently place the egg yolks in the bowl of salt water and let it sit for 10 minutes. Gently remove the yolks and place them into another small bowl; carefully cover the yolks with 1 cup of olive oil.

2. In a large saucepan, bring 2 quarts of salted water to a boil. Add the leek, blanch for 2 minutes, then remove and pat dry. Trim away the ends and the dark green parts and discard (or reserve for a future use).

Thinly slice the white and light green parts and set them aside.

3. In the same water, add the rice and cook, stirring occasionally, until tender, approximately 20 minutes. Strain and let cool.

4. In a sauté pan, heat 1 tablespoon of olive oil over medium-high heat until shimmering. Remove the sausage from its casing, crumble, and add to the pan. Breaking it up with a spoon, flatten the meat out so it gets crispy. Once the sausage begins to brown, after 3 to 5 minutes, stir in the sliced leeks, shrimp, and garlic. Season with a pinch of salt and pepper.

5. Stir in the cooked rice, tossing to coat it. Gently stir in the tomato puree and finally the chili and parsley.

6. To serve, divide the rice evenly among four serving dishes. Remove the egg yolks from the oil with a slotted spoon and add to the top of each dish. Sprinkle with chives.

FENNEL SAUSAGE

The revered pig has been a hallmark of il Buco since the early days. For Alberto, the animals of the family barnyard are an integral part of the Umbrian culture, and the pig plays a huge role in this landlocked region. Bernardo Flores has carried this torch for so many years at il Buco that it is second nature to him. Yet as much as he and we would love to share our salumi recipes with all of you, the reality would require a prohibitive amount of equipment and infrastructure. But making fresh sausages is easy. So here is a rela- tively simple recipe that will yield indelible delight for the adventurous cook and make the Black Rice with Sausage & Shrimp (page 77) all the more delectable. At Alimentari we dry the sausages to make caccia- torini, but these fresh ones can be simply grilled in their casings or emptied from their casings and added to any number of pasta dishes to great effect. The fennel pollen is the key ingredient and adds the subtle flavor that sings here. Follow in Bernardo's footsteps and try on your *norcino* skills with this recipe.

Serves 8 to 10

4 pounds pork shoulder, cut into ¼-inch cubes
2 tablespoons kosher salt
1 tablespoon fennel pollen
1 tablespoon Aleppo pepper
2 tablespoons whole fennel seeds
5 tablespoons fresh oregano leaves, finely chopped
4 garlic cloves
3 tablespoons ice-cold water
1 sausage casing

Special equipment needed: stand mixer with meat grinder and sausage stuffer attachment

1. Mix all the ingredients together except the casing. Place in the freezer until the meat reaches 32°F.

2. Once chilled, grind through a ¼-inch meat grinder plate attached to the meat grinder.

3. Divide the meat in half, regrind one half. Then mix both halves together.

4. Rinse the casing well with cold water and feed onto a large tube of the sausage stuffer attachment on a stand mixer. Tie a knot at the end of the casing and pierce it gently with the tip of a toothpick. Pass the meat from the stuffer into the casing, making sure the meat is densely packed. Once you have used all the meat, twist the sausages into 4-inch lengths. Tie off the casing after the last sausage. Trim excess casing. Using a toothpick, prick the sausage a few times per link.

5. Roll the sausage into a spiral. Grill immediately, refrigerate for up to 5 days, or freeze for up to 3 months.

"In our many hours of work together on the salumi program at Alimentari, Bernardo became my spiritual brother. We protected that place and the salumi like a baby."

—CHRISTOPHER LEE

IV

L'OLIO

There are so many ways to fall in love with olive oil: drizzled on a slice of grilled bread or crisscrossed atop just-picked tomatoes, or shimmering hot in a pan, ready to receive garlic and herbs. Versatile and accommodating, good olive oil holds so many notes, it's hard to think they can be contained in this unctuous liquid of varying hues from gold to green. Spicy, grassy, nutty, bold, buttery, every drop is a symphony of flavor.

This might come as a surprise, because so much of the olive oil consumed in America is a shadow of the real thing, a denatured industrial product of obscure origin that tastes like . . . nothing. On the other hand, a good olive oil—cold pressed, freshly harvested, made from a single varietal—rivals wine in complexity and nuance. Just like wine, the origin of the oil—the soil, the breeze, the people who grow and harvest the olives—is just as important as the levels of acidity or, say, the phenolic compounds. A good olive oil comes from somewhere but can seduce anywhere.

The first time I fell in love with it was in Umbria almost twenty years ago. I found myself in Foligno,

naturally, thanks to Alberto. He had been away from home for more than eight years and was beginning to miss his roots. Mostly he was missing his most basic raw materials. He had grown up in this land, played among the trees, followed his nonna through so many harvests, and so this olive oil was a part of him too. Olive oil ran through Alberto's veins. Even before we opened il Buco, he had spent hours furiously chasing down leads to high-quality olive oil through the streets and shelves of Manhattan. But none of the options passed muster. I can still see his face recoiling in disgust when he tasted the pallid blended oils that passed themselves off as extra virgin. The olive oil that Alberto was after was the end product of centuries of tradition and love. I have to admit, at first, I didn't get it. But standing in the groves outside of Foligno, I understood at once.

The first stop was the mill of Claudio Metelli, whose oil was the first imported to il Buco. At that time he was harvesting in November and milling with a traditional stone mill. We stopped for a visit, and I stood in awe as the fluorescent green liquid was poured over a slice of toasted bread. The flavor sensation was irresistible. I think I ate an entire loaf that afternoon. I was so inspired, yet I still had not experienced the harvest itself. I vowed to return the following year. By that time Alberto had conjured the help of a dear friend, Marco Pandolfi, and his father, il Conte, to produce the oil for il Buco.

The Pandolfi are a noble family, and though Marco's father, whom everyone called il Conte, the Count, was the last title holder, the estate had been in the family for ten generations and remained so. This land was Marco's, and the olive trees were as much a part of his family as the foreboding relatives staring down from their portraits in the ancient stone house on the hill above the groves.

When I first met Marco he was standing among his groves of gnarled olive trees in San Sebastiano, a subdistrict of Foligno, Umbria. He stood tall in the sunlight, with wavy black hair and piercing blue eyes, and the shadows of the branches danced upon his features. All around us, gentle hills rose and fell under a clear blue sky. The groves in the valleys nearby flickered silver and green as the leaves moved in the breeze, and the autumn air was thick with the distinct smell of olive trees. We connected immediately over a love of horses, sailing, and the surrounding nature. I was always a welcome guest at the San Sebastiano estate, whether for his wedding to Alberta in 2001, the arrival of his son, Guglielmo, or for countless harvests. My arrival was usually met with a gallop through the groves on his beautiful horses, Brio and Charme, Marco riding beside me as our horses took off up the hills and down into the valleys between the olive trees.

The trees on Marco's estate were Moraiolo olives, a cultivar, or variety, known for their strong yet well-balanced flavor that could compete with the local game—like *cinghiale*, or wild boar—that makes up the cuisine of central Italy. Though the Moraiolo first came from Tuscany, thanks to the altitude, the climate, and the soil, olives from Foligno are among the most prized in all of Italy. Since the 1600s, when the Pope ordered groves planted, these hills have borne olive trees and thus olive oil.

When we visited Marco, like many other small grove owners, the Pandolfi used the town's municipal mill to press their olives every autumn. Though it wasn't for sale—perhaps because it wasn't for sale—il Conte produced olive oil with a perfectionist's touch. Every step along the way, he chose quality over quantity. He spent hours walking through the groves with his right-hand man, Renato, surveying each branch and pruning for perfection. No pesticides or herbicides were ever used. He still harvested by hand, using plastic rakes to scrape the olives from the branches, though a mechanical harvest yields much more product. Olive trees left unmolested by mechanical pickers, according to the Count, are happier. I would say it would be hard to be unhappy in those groves.

Il Conte found a kindred spirit in Alberto, who suggested moving to an October harvest when the smaller, less ripe olives yielded scarcer oil, lower in acidity and higher in polyphenols or antioxidants. The first season of experimentation proved the point in spades, and this pungent, herbaceous, yet elegant oil became the foundation for us at il Buco.

In 1999 I did return to Umbria to experience my first harvest. Being a filmmaker, I decided to bring along a cameraman and film this first-time event. With my dear friend Edgar Gil in tow, we flew to Italy. The stories Alberto had told were so vivid, yet nothing matched the real-life experience. The Count and Marco opened their world to me and I eagerly stepped in.

RIGHT: Donna and Marco Pandolfi in olive grove, Serra Alta

Il Conte e Marco Pandolfi-Elmi

Il Conte e Marco Pandolfi-Elmi

During *la raccolta*, or harvest, a small group of *folignati*, as the locals are called, gathered to harvest the olives on the Pandolfi estate. Many were in their sixties and seventies, with fingers as gnarled as the trees themselves and faces as wizened as their trunks. Alberto had these same crooked fingers, which he told me came from generations of his family members working the land, harvesting with the seasons. Women dressed in the floral aprons of a *casalinga* (housewife), with their hair gathered back in kerchiefs, and gray-haired, sun-crinkled men the age of Alberto's father gathered in the groves to pick. Bearing long wooden ladders on their shoulders, they threw their nets on the ground around each tree, then headed up among the branches to strip the olives, by hand or with small handheld rakes. It was hard physical labor, but as the olives tumbled, some green, some slightly purple, into the nets below, the group sang old songs of love that had been sung for generations. It was part reunion, part reenactment, part labor of love, a way to reconnect with the bygone traditions of their youth. Some of these folks—Olga, Renato, Oriana, Luigi—would become friends I'd follow up with as the years went by, visiting them and their families whenever I was in town. Zia Olga would greet me eagerly at her home in the small village of Cancellara, where we would often take a tour of her chicken coop and taste the fruits of her most recent foraging in the hills above her home with her daughter, Pasqualina. On my last visit three years ago with my nephew, Danny, she cried tears of joy when she saw me. She was over eighty and in the early stages of dementia, but she sang the familiar songs of the harvest, and we laughed together. That would be our last visit. She passed away last August.

For Alberto and the Pandolfi family and many Italians, producing olive oil is a source of great pride. It's as integral a part of their culture and history as the churches are, dominating even the smallest community. A life without olive oil is a life without soul.

Marco took it seriously too, as seriously as he could. But by the time we met him, the younger Pandolfi was making his living as an antiques dealer. His father was in his seventies, and the groves, which had borne fruit for centuries, faced an uncertain future. So many of the youth were no longer interested in harvesting, and the crews were made up more and more of immigrants who needed to be integrated into the culture and community and trained. It was also difficult to depend on an outside mill to press one's olives, and issues of trust and oil mixing were rampant.

At a certain point we put our heads together with Marco and decided to help him build his own mill. Though it sounds daunting and expensive, the mechanics of olive oil production are shockingly simple. The olives are ground into a paste, and the paste is then pressed; water separates from the oil and olive residue. The most important issue is not adding heat to the process; thus the term *cold pressed*. By this time the technology had also advanced rapidly. A company called Rapanelli, based in Umbria, had developed a new technology called Sinolea, operating on the simple principle in which steel blades penetrated the fruit, separating the oil from water without added heat. A simple centrifuge spun the remainder of the pulp to extract the remainder of the oil. Like most extractions, the gentler and more patient the process, the purer the product. To our good fortune, Rapanelli was offering smaller machinery that catered to smaller production. To some extent, we were self-interested. We knew we needed the highest-quality olive oil at il Buco, and not just any olive oil, but an olive oil with a mission to help a small producer do the right thing. Here was our chance to guarantee our supply, to reach out from our still-small kitchen in the belly of Manhattan into the hills of Umbria and actually make a difference, and to help a friend. In 2000, we completed the small state-of-the-art *frantoio* on the Pandolfi estate. Soon, vibrant, almost neon green oil was streaming out of the press and into dark-hued glass bottles destined for il Buco.

LEFT: Scenes from Donna's documentary film "La Raccolta": Count Pandolfi and son, Marco; the Count and Renato; Olga and Oriana harvesting; Luigi; olive mill details FOLLOWING: Marco Pandolfi's olive grove, Serra Alta, Umbria

Over the years, our circle of olive oil makers has expanded to include farmers like Alberto Galluffo in Trapani, Sicily. An olive oil consultant, Alberto has been perfecting monocultivar oils from western Sicily since 1995. There, on the extreme western tip of Sicily, buffeted by the Mediterranean winds, Alberto has built a small farm in the Valli Trapanesi. Naturally, Alberto's oil is much different from Marco's. Olive oil, like olives, belongs to a region. Each cultivar has developed in accordance and harmony with its home. So whereas Moraiolo (from Umbria) pairs with the bravura cuisine of central Italy, the Biancolilla and Cerasuolo and Norcellara culvitars that dot Alberto's groves, on the other hand, are subtler in nature. The oil of the Biancolilla olives—so called because of their dappled white-and-lilac bodies—is the most delicate and is often used in blends. Alberto was determined to produce a monocultivar of this oil to fully appreciate its delicate characteristics, which complement ceviche and crudo often caught just kilometers from the grove. Cerasuolo is slightly more robust; the root of the word is from *ciliegia*, or cherry, and thus it is grown among the fruit and vegetable trees a bit more inland and has notes of freshly cut grass and even tomatoes. It's the perfect oil to dress a salad or in which to roast vegetables. At il Buco, we use the Nocellara for our gratis table service, as it is the most plentiful and hearty and therefore less expensive to produce.

Olive oil is a perishable product. Unlike a wine, it gets flatter, not better, with age. So it must be used, and we use more than 1,000 liters every year. As the universe of il Buco has grown, I've found more producers throughout Italy with whom to partner. But regardless of the varietal or the farmer, I always look for producers like il Conte and Alberto Galluffo:

men and women driven by passion and devotion to quality. I look for producers who seek to do the least possible to the best possible ingredients—producers who respect the olive by not subjecting it to heat or to chemical processes that wring from the fruit and pits every last drop of oil, producers who care too much to blend last year's oil with this year's oil or mindlessly mix a hodgepodge of varietals. When I taste an olive oil, slurping it loudly to let the air carry the flavor through my mouth and nose, I want the land to come through with all its spicy and strong notes. I am looking for taste, and a story too.

Over the years, I've returned again and again to the hills of Foligno. I return to check on the groves and because Marco has become almost family. We still occasionally gallop through the rows of olive trees on horseback, like we've done year after year, eye-level with the olives on the branches, purple and green. Marco's hair is salt and pepper now and his eyes a bit more wrinkled. His father, the Count, passed away in 2016. But I know these olive trees will continue to bear fruit and that this oil will be enjoyed for years to come.

When you walk into il Buco Alimentari, you'll see rows of bottles and tins of our olive oil on the walls. Walk farther back, and you'll see it used in nearly everything we make. Eat at il Buco or from our recipes and you'll taste olive oil given its proper due. Along with salt and vinegar, it is the foundation of our kitchen. But to fully understand what makes olive oil so magical, just imagine Olga perched atop a ladder, singing ancient songs in her warbling voice, songs she's been singing since she was a girl, and hear the responses of the her fellow folignati as they answer in song as the sun sets over the groves of Foligno.

CLOCKWISE FROM TOP LEFT: Uppello; Marco Pandolfi; olive trees, Serra Alta; the hills of Serra Alta; ruin, olive grove; olive oil cruet

V

ANTIPASTI DI MARE

SCALLOP CRUDO

In the coastal towns of Italy, where fish markets crowd the ports and the daily catch glistens in the sun, *crudo di pesce* has been served for centuries. *Crudo* means "raw" but the preparation isn't as simple as that. A crudo is a delicate and fascinating interplay among the fish, citrus, oil, and, usually, a bit of spice. The same can be said for *ceviche*, a similar preparation with South American rather than Mediterranean roots. The acid—often from lemon, sometimes from vinegar—denatures the proteins of the fish, preserving its silken texture. Especially in shellfish like scallops and razor clams, this is key. What's more, the natural sweetness of the seafood is more pronounced with the help of fresh herbal elements. After a quick cure to firm up the flesh, even oily fish like mackerel benefit from this less-is-more approach.

The tender sweet flesh of scallops makes them perfect for this simple yet quite sophisticated preparation. As so often is the case with crudi, it's the exchange and interplay of citric acid with the seafood that brings to the dish its bright pop. The basil, meanwhile, brings an herbaceous hint, rounding out the flavors. If you can find a seafood shop with the scallops still in their shells, buy these. The shells add a beautiful flourish at the table, connecting you to the origins of these elegant creatures.

Serves 4

8 very fresh live-in-shell scallops (or roughly 1 pound of U-10 scallops)
3 tablespoons cold Meyer lemon juice (from approximately 2 lemons)
2 tablespoons extra virgin olive oil
1 tablespoon coarse sea salt
10 whole basil leaves (opal preferably)

1. If the scallops are live and in their shells, pry them apart with a shucking knife. Running the blade between the meat and the shell, separate the entire scallop from its shell. Using your fingers, remove the white edible part of the scallop from the inedible frill and gut. Rinse the scallops well under running water, tossing vigorously for 2 to 3 minutes. Clean and reserve shells.

2. Pat scallops dry and slice into ⅛-inch-thick coins.

3. Prepare the sauce by blending the Meyer lemon juice in a blender at full speed. Then slowly add olive oil. The sauce should have a consistency slightly thicker than olive oil (the cold juice makes for the best emulsification).

4. To serve, divide the scallop slices equally among eight shells, approximately 4 to 5 slices per shell. Spoon the Meyer lemon–oil mixture atop, season with sea salt, and garnish with basil leaves.

OCTOPUS CARPACCIO

Carpaccio is often served raw. In fact, when the preparation was invented by Giuseppe Cipriani at Harry's Bar in Venice in the 1950s, it was so named because the red and white tones of the raw sliced beef reminded Cipriani of paintings by the fifteenth-century Venetian painter Vittore Carpaccio. Since then, carpaccio has come to mean almost anything sliced thinly and served with olive oil, acid, and salt. Octopus is not best raw, and so in this version, we boil the octopus first in a court bouillon to both tenderize it and endow it with flavor. Then we form a basic octopus terrine, which is then sliced thin. It's a lot of work, but the dish is as stunning as Cipriani's first carpaccio, a masterpiece of flavor, texture, and visuals. This dish often graced the menus in the early days of il Buco, sometimes with some raw fava beans thrown on top. It lost none of its charm years later in Ibiza, when we reintroduced it, drizzled with our lemon Biancolilla, surrounded by sea and sun.

Serves 4

1 bay leaf
Peel of 1 lemon
1 sprig rosemary
1 sprig thyme
1 teaspoon whole black peppercorns
1 tablespoon coarse sea salt
1 (2-pound) octopus
3 tablespoons extra virgin olive oil, divided
½ tablespoon salted capers, rinsed
Zest of ½ orange
Leaves from 2 sprigs cilantro
Aleppo pepper or Urfa biber to taste
Fiore di sale (or best quality sea salt),
    for finishing

1. Bring 2 quarts water and the bay leaf, lemon peel, rosemary, thyme, peppercorns, and salt to a boil in a large pot. (Make sure there is sufficient room because the octopus releases a lot of water as it cooks.) Once the water is boiling, add the octopus, bring to a simmer, and allow to cook for 30 to 35 minutes until tender.

2. Remove the octopus from water, let cool slightly, then cut the tentacles from the head. Discard the head or retain for another use.

3. Line a loaf pan with a sheet of plastic wrap. Layer the whole tentacles, alternating thick and thin, then cover completely with plastic wrap. Place a cardboard cutout over the top, and then an empty bottle of olive oil or a heavy can to weigh it down. Once compacted, freeze the octopus terrine overnight.

4. When ready to serve, heat 1 tablespoon of olive oil in a small sauté pan. Fry capers for 4 to 5 minutes until crispy. Drain and set aside.

5. Remove the octopus from the freezer and the loaf pan and remove the plastic wrap. Using the sharpest knife you have, shave the pressed octopus into very thin slices.

6. To serve, lay the octopus slices on a large platter. Drizzle with the remaining olive oil. Top with the fried capers, orange zest, cilantro leaves, Aleppo pepper or Urfa biber, and fiore di sale to taste.

RAZOR CLAM CEVICHE

Though these long narrow clams—they look like a straight razor—didn't start to appear on menus in New York until about ten years ago, they've long been prized in Asian cuisine, as well as Spanish and Italian. In Italy and Spain, they're often grilled or broiled, but I find those preparations a bit rubbery and sometimes end up with remnant sand in my mouth. But when Justin Smillie first put them on the menu at Alimentari in this iteration, I was sold. I find their sweet subtle flavor is best showcased as a ceviche, with only the delicate acid of the finger limes to "cook" them. Naturally, a delicate olive oil like our Biancolilla and squeeze of lemon finishes the ceviche perfectly.

Serves 4

20 razor clams, live in shell
5 finger limes, whole
3 tablespoons Meyer lemon juice
3 tablespoons extra virgin olive oil
1 tablespoon fine sea salt
2 teaspoons chopped chives
Espelette pepper to taste

1. If the razor clams are not yet purged—ask your purveyor if they are—soak them in cold water for 20 minutes to remove any sand and grime. Then pop open the clams by running a paring or butter knife between the shells. Trim the clam by removing and discarding the belly portion, which is dark brown, leaving the meat, pearlescent and creamy, untouched. Run a knife between the flesh of the clam and the shell, then remove the meat. Slice on a bias into ¼-inch strips. Clean and reserve the shells.

2. Squeeze out four finger limes into a small bowl. Add the Meyer lemon juice and olive oil. Mix gently with a spoon so as not to break the juice vesicles, also called the pearls, of the lime.

3. Lay out four half shells per person. Fill each with razor clam slices, between 6 and 7, then sprinkle with sea salt. Spoon the citrus mixture over each shell of sliced clam, then garnish with chives and Espelette pepper. Thinly slice the remaining finger lime and scatter the slices atop the clams. Serve immediately.

"If I could reserve two seats, it would be the corner of the bar. From there I could reminisce, laugh, and know I am somewhere perfect."

—MELANIE DUNEA

MACKEREL CRUDO WITH PLUMS

Fresh Spanish mackerel is one of my favorite fish. Aside from its wonderfully meaty texture with a slight oiliness, the flavor is light and mellow when it's fresh. As a blue fish, it is extremely high in omega-3s, as are anchovies and sardines and all fish in this category. In Ibiza mackerel are plentiful; this preparation from Bottega il Buco is fun and easy. The shiso and horseradish play against the slightly sweet plum to counteract the oily quality of the fish. If you prepare this on a bright summer day, you might be transported to a little Spanish paradise.

Hamachi, also called yellowtail or Japanese amberjack, is a fish with a buttery texture and mild flavor that makes it a perfect alternative for the mackerel in this preparation.

Serves 4

Zest of 2 limes
½ cup fine sea salt, plus additional for finishing
½ cup sugar
⅓ pound horse mackerel fillet (or hamachi; see headnote)
2 purple or yellow plums
4 tablespoons extra virgin olive oil
½ bunch dill
¼ teaspoon freshly shaved horseradish
Micro shiso leaves, to garnish

1. Mix together the lime zest, salt, and sugar to make a quick cure. Place the mackerel in the mixture, cover completely, and let sit refrigerated for 20 minutes.

2. Meanwhile, slice the plums into ⅛-inch-thick slices.

3. Combine the olive oil and dill in a small saucepan and heat over very low heat for 30 minutes to infuse. Let cool completely.

4. After the mackerel is cured, remove the translucent outer membrane from the skin side of the fish. Rinse the mackerel, pat dry, and cut into ¼-inch slices.

5. To plate, alternate slices of the mackerel and plums (alternating colors if using both purple and yellow). Garnish with the shaved horseradish and shiso. Top with dill-infused olive oil and additional salt to taste.

BOTTARGA WITH SHAVED CELERY

Salty, sweet, creamy, and delicate, bottarga di muggine is one of my go-to ingredients. Resembling *membrillo* (quince paste) in both color and texture, bottarga is made from the air-cured ovarian sacs of grey mullet. I have to admit that when Alberto first introduced me to this product on a trip to Oristano, the sleepy sun-washed city in Sardegna, I wasn't enthusiastic. ("Air-cured ovarian sacs" were not something I intuitively knew to be delicious.) But, as I discovered, bottarga combines both a subtle brininess and a creamy texture. Whether tossed with spaghetti or as here, sliced thin and accompanied by the fresh crunch of celery and a mild olive oil, it adds a whisper of the sea, a sweetness touched with a slight pungency.

Serves 4

5 celery stalks, including leaves
Juice of ½ lemon (about 1½ tablespoons)
Sea salt, for finishing
4 ounces bottarga di muggine
3 tablespoons mild olive oil, such as Biancolilla

1. Remove and reserve the outer leaves of the celery and slice the stalks thinly on a bias. Place on a serving plate.

2. Season with the lemon juice and a pinch of sea salt.

3. Using a sharp paring knife, slice the bottarga on the bias into thin strips, no more than ⅛ inch thick, and carefully lay it atop the celery.

4. Drizzle everything with olive oil and garnish with a few celery leaves. Serve immediately.

"I always thought that what made il Buco so special was that it was imperfect, never quite finished. And, for heaven's sake, they were always selling the furniture!"
—BOB GUCCIONE JR.

GRILLED CALAMARI

There are a couple of summer staples I rely on when guests come to visit my house in East Hampton's Springs: the small, sweet baby peppers from the wonderful farmstands and the fresh local calamari from Stuart's seafood shop. Once in a while they actually offer the calamari cleaned, which saves lots of time and mess. I usually throw some peppers on one half of the grill and these calamari on the other. Both take about the same time to cook and both are perfect ways to begin an evening feast. The only trick here is that you'll want a grill rack or tray so that the little calamari tentacles don't fall through the grill. They're the best part, and you don't want to lose them. A healthy drizzle of olive oil, salt, pepper, and the best local cherry tomatoes make the perfect start to an early summer feast.

Serves 4 to 6

1½ pounds medium squid, cleaned
2 garlic cloves, finely chopped
1 tablespoon chopped fresh oregano
1 teaspoon fine sea salt, plus more for finishing
Freshly ground black pepper to taste
2 tablespoons olive oil, divided, plus more
    for finishing
½ pint cherry tomatoes, halved widthwise
    (or quartered depending on the size)
1 bunch basil, torn into pieces, or chopped coarsely

1. Place the squid bodies and tentacles on a wide platter or in a large bowl. Season with the garlic, oregano, salt, and pepper and drizzle with 1 tablespoon olive oil. Toss to coat. Cover and let marinate for approximately 15 minutes.

2. In a small bowl, mix the halved cherry tomatoes, 1 tablespoon olive oil, basil, salt, and pepper.

3. Preheat grill over high heat. Place a grill tray on the grill to preheat as well, until the tray is ripping hot. (If you don't have a tray, proceed with cooking directly on the grill, just be careful that the tentacles do not fall between the grates.)

4. Place the squid on the grill tray in a single layer. Cook, flipping once, until the flesh is opaque and slightly charred but still tender, 2 to 3 minutes per side. Divide the bodies and the tentacles onto plates and top with the halved tomato and basil mixture. Finish with salt and olive oil to taste, and serve immediately.

"The bookish should not miss the exquisite edition of Poe on the shelves by the door to the wine cellar, where this old sommelier's heart is trapped forever, just like the dude in 'The Cask of Amontillado.'"

—WILLIAM FITCH

SEARED TUNA
WITH FENNEL POLLEN

All across the Mediterranean, you'll find some variation of a tuna and white bean dish, though the tuna is most often cured in olive oil. This is a riff on the classic with fresh seared tuna, rare inside and crusted with wild fennel pollen.

Alberto chose corona beans for this dish, reminiscent of the local beans that line the banks of the Menotre River, which runs through his hometown, Foligno. These beans have a lovely meatiness and, like gigantes and butter, are among the larger white beans. In this rendition, it's important that the beans blister on the outside and retain a creaminess inside.

The final touch is the fennel pollen, which grows wild throughout the region, which Alberto was crazy about, and which nearly bankrupted us. Back in 1996, no one in New York City knew what it was. The process of its cultivation is arduous: the flowers must be picked, dried atop linen, then beaten to release the pollen from the petals. The result is a fine powder with a subtle fennel flavor. Alberto hired a score of *casalinghe*, housewives, from Gubbio to produce the pollen and sent 100 kilos to the restaurant. For years, we were working off our pollen debt. But we found when we dusted the tuna with the pollen *before* we seared it, the flavor transformed into something sublime, slightly floral with a subtle nuttiness. An il Buco classic was born.

Serves 4

2 cups dried corona beans
4 bay leaves
4 garlic cloves (2 whole and 2 minced)
2 sprigs rosemary
2 teaspoons sea salt, divided, plus more to finish
3 tablespoons extra virgin olive oil, divided, plus
   more for drizzling
12 ounces ahi big eye tuna, sushi grade
3 tablespoons fennel pollen

1. Soak the corona beans in 6 cups of cold water overnight, or at least 8 hours.

2. When ready to cook the beans, drain them and place into a large pot, along with the bay leaves, 2 whole garlic cloves, rosemary, and 1 teaspoon of salt. Add water until the beans are covered and bring to a boil over medium heat. Once boiling, turn down to a simmer and cook uncovered until the beans are tender, about 40 to 45 minutes. Drain the cooked beans, discarding the liquid and aromatics.

3. In a small sauté pan over medium heat, heat 2 tablespoons of the olive oil until shimmering. Add the minced garlic, stirring until golden but not browned. Add the corona beans, giving them a good blister in the pan, then turn off the heat and toss to coat. Set aside.

4. Generously salt the tuna with the remaining teaspoon and dust with fennel pollen on all sides. Place a sauté pan over medium-high heat and add the remaining 1 tablespoon of the olive oil. Sear the tuna, turning once, until a golden crust forms, 1 to 2 minutes per side.

5. To serve, slice the seared tuna into four portions and arrange next to the corona beans. Garnish with a drizzle of olive oil and a sprinkling of sea salt.

GRILLED OCTOPUS
WITH CHICKPEAS

When *New York Times* restaurant critic Pete Wells asked in his three-star review of Alimentari, "Is it crazy to fall for a restaurant because of a handful of chickpeas?" these were the chickpeas he had in mind. "Tasting one was like encountering a goldfinch if the only birds you'd ever seen were pigeons." And with that, this dish by Justin Smillie was endeared to me forever. Since we opened, Alberto had been championing the chickpeas we imported directly from Cuore Verde in Umbria. As for the octopus itself, Chuck Close, a twenty-year regular, is such a fan we've never been able to take it off the menu without fielding his complaints. So it's thanks to Chuck, to Alberto, and, of course, to Justin, that Pete walked out that night in love with il Buco Alimentari and our chickpeas.

Serves 4

5 tablespoons extra virgin olive oil, divided
1 white onion, peeled and halved
1 bulb fennel, quartered
1 garlic bulb, halved
1 teaspoon whole black peppercorns
1 bottle dry white wine
2 tablespoons sea salt, plus 1 teaspoon, divided
1 (6-pound) octopus
1½ cups dried chickpeas, preferably Umbrian,
    soaked overnight in room temperature water
4 fresh bay leaves
2 tablespoons salted capers, rinsed and drained
Juice of 1 lemon
¼ cup chopped parsley
½ bunch chives, finely chopped (about ⅓ cup)

1. Heat 2 tablespoons of olive oil in a large stockpot over medium heat until it shimmers. Then add the onion, fennel, and garlic and cook for 6 to 8 minutes. Add the black peppercorns, wine, 2 tablespoons salt, and 8 cups of water. Bring the liquid to a simmer, then add the octopus. Cook 1 hour, or until the octopus is tender. Remove the octopus from the liquid. Separate the head from the tentacles, discarding the head or reserving for another use. Set aside the tentacles.

2. Meanwhile, drain the chickpeas and transfer them to a large stockpot. Add enough water to cover them by approximately 3 inches. Add the bay leaves and the remaining teaspoon salt, bring to a boil, then lower to a simmer for 40 to 50 minutes, until the chickpeas are tender but still retain their texture. Drain and place in a medium bowl.

3. Heat 1 tablespoon of the olive oil over medium heat in a small sauté pan. Lightly fry the capers, 3 to 4 minutes. Pour the contents of the pan into the chickpeas and stir in the lemon juice and parsley. Taste and season with salt. Set aside.

4. Cut the tentacles on the bias into 1½-inch slices but leave whole if small. Heat a large skillet over medium-high heat with the remaining 2 tablespoons of olive oil. Sear the octopus, suction side down, until charred, then flip and continue cooking, 4 to 5 minutes total.

5. To serve, equally divide the chickpeas among four plates. Place the octopus atop the chickpeas, then finish with sea salt, chives, and a dash of olive oil.

VI

IL PANE

————

The journey of il Buco's bread starts every morning at 2:30 in Bay Ridge, a working-class neighborhood deep in the heart of Brooklyn. That's where Sheena Otto, our head baker, wakes up in the darkness, kisses her baby daughter on the forehead, her husband on his cheek, and begins the long commute to her subterranean bakery at Alimentari. She takes the shuttle to the R to the D train, then walks north from Houston Street until she hits Great Jones.

At 4 she is the first to arrive in the predawn light. Occasionally she sees revelers from the night before, wobbling unsteadily on the cobblestones.

Baking is a waiting game, a matter of planning and patience. It's a discipline in which one must make peace with time. Time is what transforms the raw ingredients, almost absurdly basic, into the delicious, airy, deeply flavored loaves lining the shelves of Alimentari every morning. Flour, water, yeast, salt, time, heat, and the human hand—bread is a language with a limited vocabulary but unlimited expression. Ever since we started baking bread at il Buco, our mantra has been to let time do her work. Like everything else here, we spend lavishly and work tirelessly to procure the best ingredients and then stand back and let them shine.

From the very first day we opened the doors at il Buco, Alberto and I were passionate about bread. "Bread, water, and wine," he said, "these are the basics, and they must be of the best quality." More passionate than knowledgeable, our first experiments were simple. Alberto was rightly concerned about the world wheat crisis, the devastating effect of industrialization due to large companies like

LEFT: Grain fields, Caltanissetta, Italy

Monsanto, which led to the destruction of wheat as we knew it. He was committed to finding an unpolluted grain source. We shipped over an Austrian mill and began grinding farro to flour for grissini, those wonderfully crisp breadsticks that start a meal. But because we needed more bread, Alberto called his friends from Foligno to send our favorite spelt loaves over via air mail. Economical it wasn't, nor was the solution sustainable. We did, however, have the best bread in the city for a short spell.

It was with the creation of Alimentari that we found the platform we needed to have a true bread program. In 2010, while construction was in full swing, we hired our first baker, a talented mercurial jiujitsu fighter from Gascony named Kamel Saci, who was "wasting away" in Orlando in a more commercial bakery and was recommended by a local baker friend. He longed to get back to the artisan production for which he was trained in his native France, where a jiujitsu injury had led first to an apprenticeship to a Parisian baker and then to falling in love with the craft. When he arrived, Kamel laid the foundation for our naturally leavened bread program, turning out golden loaves of ciabatta, elongated baguettes with an airy crumb and sturdy crusts called filone, small sweet doughnuts called bomboloni, and rounds of sourdough that still bore the rings of the proofing basket on their crust.

Kamel left in the spring of 2016, and the search for his replacement began. New York is a city of eight million loaves, but finding a baker who could keep up with il Buco's high demand, who shared our swanlike mindset (endlessly busy under the water, graceful above), and who had the passion to essentially become a nun, or monk, for bread, was a heavy task. And to be honest, the first time I auditioned Sheena, I wasn't impressed. Sheena, who had been recommended by Justin's chef de cuisine Victoria Blamey, had baked six misshapen, underproofed, rock-hard loaves—a raisin loaf, a seed loaf, and an olive bread—in our kitchen. I tried to be positive. "The flavor is great," I said. Sheena, who was clearly nervous, was crestfallen and very apologetic.

But two days later, she came in with two of the most beautiful loaves of bread I had ever seen: a multigrain and a filone. She handed them to me and said, "Look, I just wanted to show you I'm not a complete loser. This is what I wanted to make." And as soon as I tore apart the filone, I knew we had found our head baker. It was light and airy, with a dark brown crust.

Today, along with Roberto and Alberto and Bernardo, Sheena has become part of the fabric at il Buco. A former investigator for New York Police Department's Civilian Complaint Review Board, ten years ago she grew tired of investigating dirty cops and turned her avocation into a profession. She started at a small Palestinian deli near her home in Bay Ridge but, through toughness, persistence, and talent, moved on to Amy's Bread, where she worked as an overnight baker for two years, and then to Atera, a fine dining Nordic restaurant, where she worked alongside Victoria Blamey. By the time we met her, Sheena was the sous chef in charge of twenty bakers managing the wholesale division at the well-respected bakery Bien Cuit. Something about her story resonated with me. We were both driven by passion and fate and succeeded through hard work and kismet. Sheena doesn't look fierce. She's small, with cherubic cheeks, thick glasses, and hair kept hidden by a bandana, but she's tough as nails. She has worked tirelessly for the past five years to make her dream of being a head baker come true.

Sheena arrives thirty minutes before the rest of the baking crew to still her mind. She stands before her workspace, a large wooden table tucked in the back of the kitchen, past the pasta station and the butcher room. A deck oven is to her left. In baking, she says, anything you bring in from the outside world will make its way to the bread. That goes for anger and sadness, impatience and anxiety. Dough is a porous thing. Before it is baked, before the crust forms, it is a living thing, susceptible to the environment.

RIGHT: Sheena Otto, head baker

Bread at il Buco isn't just a staple. We go through 300 to 350 loaves a day. It's a core element to nearly everything we do. It is the vehicle for our pizzas, the structure of our panini, the platform for the crostini, the complement to our olive oil. It appears not just on its own but as an element in the *Pappa al Pomodoro* (page 155) and *Panzanella* (page 164). Over the years, we've gone deeper and deeper into exploring the subtleties of breadmaking. Today, on our shelves, you'll find a naturally fermented buckwheat rye, made with Anson Mills rye; a bourbon raisin fennel bread; a flavorful multigrain loaf with pumpkin, sunflower, sesame, and flax seeds; and my favorite, Castelvetrano olive bread. These are in addition, of course, to the classic ciabatta, filone, and focaccia.

Sheena came to baking because she loved it. And she's developed tendrils in the baking world that extend beyond our kitchen. Her philosophy begins with the commitment to highly hydrated, naturally leavened sourdoughs that are cold fermented for up to twenty-four hours to coax more complex flavor and aromas. The starters, or "mothers," are cultures made up of lactic acid bacteria and naturally occurring yeasts that live together harmoniously in, most commonly, a flour and water mixture. This culture leavens and flavors the loaves, breaking down the gluten and providing a more easily digestible product. Bakers are passionate about their "mothers," and Sheena's "mother" came from her friend Beatrice, who runs a wonderful little bakery in Barcelona. The two bakers are still tied at the hip.

Last summer, to fulfill a lifelong dream of living in Spain—before her life would shift inexorably with the arrival of her daughter, Rita—Sheena jumped on a plane and set off for Spain to assist Beatrice in her new bakery in Madrid. With her own little "bun in the oven," she spent three months in Madrid studying new techniques and expanding her horizons. During that trip, she came to visit us in Ibiza to check out our ancient grain focaccia program at Bottega il Buco in the heart of Santa Gertrudis to further explore this delicate art.

Just as we chased olive oil, salt, and balsamic vinegar from the table back to groves, salt pans, and vineyards, we've chased our loaves back from the oven to the field. In 2016, when my nephew, Danny Rubin, began working with us, Alberto found another passionate comrade in his search for ancient grains. Together the two of them traveled to Caltanisetta, the granary of Italy in the exact middle of Sicily, in search of the absolute best wheat we could find.

That's how I got to know Marco Riggi, our wheat whisperer. Marco is the son of Calagero Riggi, who in 1955 founded a flour mill in the heart of Sicily. Marco and his two brothers, Cataldo and Alessandro, now run the company, which specializes in resurrecting and fostering the cultivation of such ancient grains as perciasacchi, timilia, and russello.

On a recent summer day, Marco met us at the mill, a small building behind a row of cacti in a residential stretch of Caltanisetta. The smell of a flour mill is hard to describe, somewhere between bakery and farm. A fine white powder filled the air, visible only as the sunlight shone through the window. Here Marco's mills—handsome, heavy, mint-green metal machines—did their work, grinding the wheat germ, bran, and endosperm against a heavy burrstone. Even these millstones themselves are an act of resurrection. Marco explains the best millstones come from La Ferté-sous-Jouarre, a small French town known for its quarries and fierce fighting during the Great War. Stone-grinding flour is a much more laborious process, but it preserves the nutritional value of the wheat germ and bran as well as allowing the underlying character of the wheat to come through. The millstones of La Ferté-sous-Jouarre are of an extremely hard freshwater quartz, which made the region famous. But by the time Marco was in the market for millstones, in 2000, there were hardly any left. Marco scoured the area for months until he found one. Why spend so much effort tracking down a rare millstone? Because this glorious heirloom wheat demands it. To give us an

LEFT: Buckwheat rye loaves in proofing baskets

idea, Marco gestures for us to jump in the back of his pickup truck. We're headed for the fields.

High into the Sicilian hills we go, zipping around hairpin curves. The land opens herself up and lies before us, curves covered in golden grain. Marco works only with local farmers whom, over the years, he's convinced to cultivate these ancient, less common grains. As we bounce along the road, pavement giving way to gravel giving way to dirt, we wind higher and higher up the hillside. Finally, we come to the home of Carla, one of these farmers, who bids us follow her even higher up to her fields where she presides over a vast landscape virtually on her own, committed to producing the most sustainable grains of this ancient land.

Skull-shook and sore, we pile out of the truck just in time to see a giant thresher moving across the steep hill like some sort of mechanical mammoth. Harvesting grain on this terrain is dangerous stuff: one false move and the thresher will tumble. As we walk down a narrow lane between fields, flanked by wild caperberry bushes and sage, Marco explains that for decades these heritage grains had gone uncultivated. As the global market for flour continued to exert its pull on Sicily, more common, easier-to-grow, higher-yield wheat flourished, whereas these varietals—unfit for mass production—dwindled. It was only by finding like-minded farmers like Carla, willing to devote part of their fields to organic heirloom varieties, that Marco has been able to supply his mill. But standing at sunset, listening to the gentle whisper of wind through the wheat and the occasional bell of a grazing goat, it's easy to see the appeal. For me and for Marco. "This grain is what makes Sicily Sicily," he tells me, "it has a history here. It is from here . . . just like I am."

And so it was with Marco's wheat that we began our own little Spanish outpost on the island of Ibiza, where the day begins with the wafting aroma of nutty timilia focaccia fresh from the oven, ready for any variety of local ingredients to enhance its rich flavor. The focaccia is indeed the staple from which the menu evolves at Bottega il Buco. It's the perfect starter after a long afternoon on the beach, a great accompaniment to the tinned imported fish we bring in from the mainland and Portugal, or the soothing addition to a local fish crudo or salad or salumi plate. And now, thanks to Danny and Sheena's collaboration, we're serving that focaccia at the Alimentari counter daily as well.

For us the challenge is how to communicate the breathtaking beauty back at il Buco. On one hand, even the most ahistorically minded and jaded New Yorker can't help but appreciate the quality of the grain that shines through each loaf. Perciasacchi, for instance— so called because its small sharp kernels used to pierce the wheat sacks it came in—has a mellow, sweet flavor. Timilia, which is used locally to make a black bread in Trapani, bears a nutty flavor with a hint of cinnamon. Much of this work at il Buco falls to Sheena, who must wrestle with these unwieldy grains to showcase their natural quality. With naturally less gluten, they're harder to rise and harder to manipulate. It takes a deft hand to turn the dough into the perfect golden loaves that enhance the bread racks at Alimentari. These loaves are emblems of these small acts of heroism that Sheena shares with the producers in Caltanisetta. It is a collaboration born of an enormous respect for nature that begins in the vast grainfields of central Sicily, continues each morning at 2:30 in Bay Ridge with a kiss, and ends in the bakery on Great Jones Street.

CLOCKWISE FROM TOP LEFT: Ancient grain bread, Bottega il Buco; Donna and Joaquin in Riggi's fields, Caltanisetta; grain detail; grain thresher; Michele Fasciana in his truck; sheep in landscape, Caltanisetta; Carla La Placa, ancient grain farmer FOLLOWING: Riggi ancient grain fields, Caltanisetta

PANE, PIZZE, E CROSTINI

SOURDOUGH STARTER

As the name suggests, a sourdough starter is the key to making your own sourdough. By simply combining flour and water, the yeast in the grain is activated. As you feed the mixture with fresh flour and water, the yeast develops into a beautiful, foamy, fragrant starter. It's both a magical and simple process, the perfect introduction to baking. The bad news—if you want to call it that—is that it takes time to make your starter, patience being perhaps the most important skill a baker has to cultivate. The good news: a starter takes little oversight and lasts nearly forever—they've been known to work even when well over one hundred years old.

If your local water is chlorinated—like ours is in New York City—just leave it out on the counter for an hour so that all the chlorine dissipates. You may also use distilled water, especially if you live in an area with particularly hard water.

Note: Baking is a precision game and for that reason, the recipe below uses weight measurements rather than volume.

Day 1: Starting the Starter

50 grams organic spelt flour
50 grams cool tap water

Mix above ingredients by hand in a small bowl, scrape down the side, and cover with plastic wrap and leave overnight at room temperature.

Days 2 to 7: Refreshing the Starter (Stage 1)

Sourdough starter is alive, and just like all living things, needs "feeding," which you will do by refreshing it daily in this stage (taking a small amount of your bubbling starter mixture and mixing in a proportionate amount of flour and water). Refreshing the starter provides a food source that will keep the wild yeast alive and multiplying. In this stage, every day that the starter shows activity, you need to refresh it. As long as the starter smells reminiscent of a food (cheese, yogurt, bread, slightly alcoholic) it is safe to continue. Sometimes your starter will develop a thin brownish or graying liquid on top. This liquid is just a fermentation by-product; it should be drained and discarded, and will not have a negative effect on your starter.

If there is no activity on day 2, let the starter sit for another day at room temperature. By day 3 or 4, you should begin to see signs of activity in your starter: at first your starter will begin to bubble, then it will begin to rise, and finally as it reaches its peak and is ready to refresh, "soapy" bubbles begin to collect in the center of the starter and the center starts to dip. This means the starter has exhausted its food supply and needs to be refreshed with new flour and water.

Whether or not your starter is showing activity by day 4, you should refresh it according to this stage 1 recipe below. The remainder of the starter will be discarded. Be sure to monitor the smell of your starter, if your starter begins to smell like something you would NOT eat (paint thinner, rotting garbage), the microbiotic activity in the starter has tipped in the favor of harmful bacteria, and you should discard it and begin again.

Stage 1 Refresher:

50 grams sourdough starter mixture*
50 grams organic spelt flour
50 grams water

Mix these ingredients by hand in a small bowl, scrape down the sides, cover with plastic wrap, and leave overnight at room temperature. Continue to refresh daily with above recipe through day 7.

Days 8 to 13: Refreshing the Starter (Stage 2)

As you did in days 2 to 7, check the starter each day for activity. Once you notice your starter is bubbling and rising regularly between refreshings, it means some natural yeast has cultivated and the starter needs a different recipe to grow for its use in baking. This is stage 2, and you will follow this recipe for days 8 to 13.

You've gotten to know your starter pretty well by now, and are probably able to anticipate the time it needs between refreshings (bubbling and rising are the indicators). The timing of this will depend on many factors (climate, humidity, etc.) so follow the lead of your particular starter.

In stage 2, the starter begins to become more active, so it will need refreshing more frequently. If you don't want to wake in the middle of the night to complete multiple refreshings, you can refrigerate your starter to retard it; to do this, put it in the refrigerator after half the time it normally takes for it to reach its peak height or activity so that you still only have to refresh it once daily. For example, if your starter is ready to refresh after 12 hours at room temperature, refrigerate it after only 6 hours at room temperature, then leave it in the fridge for 18 hours (or up to 24 hours if more convenient). Then refresh it the next day.

Stage 2 Refresher:

50 grams sourdough starter mixture*
50 grams water
25 grams all-purpose flour
25 grams whole wheat flour

During days 8 to 13, refresh your active starter every day (it could be more often if you live in a warmer climate). Mix the above ingredients by hand in a small bowl, scrape down the sides, and cover with plastic wrap or a plate as a lid. Leave overnight at room temperature, or refrigerate as needed to slow the process (see above).

Day 14: Finalizing the Starter

By day 14, your sourdough starter should be bubbling and active and rising consistently between refresh-ings. If not, continue to refresh the starter using the recipe and techniques in stage 2 until you notice these patterns developing. Once your starter has reached this predictable pattern, you're ready for this step.

100 grams water
50 grams sourdough starter mixture*
50 grams all-purpose flour
50 grams whole wheat flour

Mix the above ingredients by hand in a small bowl, scrape down the sides, and cover with plastic wrap or a plate as a lid. Leave at room temperature until the starter has risen to its peak, and has begun to slightly depress in its center, the way it does when it is ready for refreshing. When this occurs, transfer the starter to the fridge.

The next day, day 15, the starter will be ready to bake bread. To use, follow the specific recipe instructions for the sourdough bread you want to bake.

Be sure to retain the remaining amount of starter for future use. This is to continue the life of your sourdough starter without having to begin again from day 1. For as long as you keep the starter, it will now need refreshing once a week using the recipe from stage 2.

For the first 13 days of creating your starter, you should discard the unused amount every time you refresh your starter. After Day 14, when your starter is active and ready for baking, you can feel free to use the leftover portion of your starter (sourdough discard) from your recipe for other baking projects, such as pancakes, or to make additional loaves of bread.

FILONE & BUCKWHEAT RYE

Filone is Sheena's take on a naturally leavened sourdough with a softer, less tangy profile than the early breads of the San Francisco bread scene that inspired her. It is our go-to loaf at Alimentari due to its versatility. With a light interior crumb and firm dark crust with complex bitter tones, it's wonderful for sandwiches and crostini.

This deeply hydrated bread also lasts for several days after baking. If you prefer a darker loaf, the buckwheat rye is earthy and easy to make by simply changing the flours and following the filone recipe. While traditional filone is oval, for the home baker, we suggest a round boule shape for baking in your dutch oven.

FILONE
Makes 1 loaf

500 grams all-purpose flour, plus additional
    for kneading as needed
350 grams room temperature water
150 grams Sourdough Starter (page 120)
12 grams fine sea salt

Oil, for greasing the bowl
Semolina flour, for dusting

Special equipment needed: stand mixer with dough hook attachment (preferred) or plastic bowl scraper; proofing basket; spray bottle

1. Combine the flour, water, and starter in the mixing bowl of a stand mixer, and, using the dough hook attachment, mix on the lowest speed for 5 minutes. Alternatively, mix in a large bowl by hand until you do not see any remaining bits of flour and the dough transforms from a shaggy mass into a smoother mass; this will take between 5 and 15 minutes.

2. Once the dough has collected into a loose, somewhat cohesive mass, scrape down the sides and the bottom of the bowl for any floury bits. Increase the mixer speed to medium and mix for another five minutes. (If making by hand, turn dough out onto a lightly floured countertop and continue to knead for another 5 minutes.) Place the dough in a lightly oiled bowl. Cover the bowl loosely with a kitchen towel and let the dough rest for 30 to 45 minutes.

3. After the resting time, put the dough back in the mixer, sprinkle the dough with the salt, and mix on the lowest speed of the mixer for a minute or two, until you cannot see or feel any granules of salt. (If mixing by hand, sprinkle the salt on top of the dough and "cut" the salt into the dough using a bowl scraper. Knead the dough for 5 minutes, or until you cannot see or feel any salt granules remaining.)

4. Remove the dough from the mixing bowl, shape into a round, and place into a lightly oiled bowl. Cover the bowl with a kitchen towel and place in a draft-free, preferably warm corner of your kitchen to proof. The dough will NOT double in size; you're looking for about a 25 percent increase in volume, and the dough should feel "puffy" and "relaxed" prior to shaping. Depending on the temperature of your kitchen, this can take anywhere from 2 to 6 hours.

5. Once proofed, remove the dough from the bowl onto a well-floured countertop and gently de-gas the dough by patting it out and popping any large bubbles. Shape into a round by folding the dough over itself, picking up the top edge, and pulling it just over the center of the dough, then, using the heel of your hand, push the dough slightly away toward the top edge. Now turn the dough counterclockwise 90 degrees and do the same thing three more times; the dough should be round and smooth. Turn the dough over and tighten the boule by gently pulling the dough toward you, using the slight friction between the dough and your countertop to further tighten the dough. Turn the boule 90 degrees and repeat three more times. Place the boule seam side up (top side down) in a proofing basket lined with semolina flour to prevent sticking. Sprinkle more semolina over the top. Loosely cover with a kitchen towel and refrigerate overnight, anywhere from 12 to 24 hours.

6. When ready to bake, preheat the oven to 450°F; put an empty 5-quart dutch oven with its lid on to preheat as well.

7. Once your oven and pot are preheated, remove the dough from the refrigerator and carefully turn it out from the basket into the dutch oven. Score the top of the dough using a sharp paring knife in any pattern you like. Using a spray bottle, spray the dough with a little water, cover with the dutch oven lid, and place entire vessel in your oven. Bake for 20 minutes.

8. Remove the lid and continue to bake for 20 to 30 minutes, or until the crust is a deep golden brown.

9. Let bread cool completely before serving.

BUCKWHEAT RYE
Makes 1 loaf

315 grams all-purpose flour
295 grams room temperature water
270 grams Sourdough Starter (page 120)
90 grams rye flour
60 grams buckwheat flour
15 grams fine sea salt
Oil, for greasing the bowl
Semolina flour, for dusting

To make the buckwheat rye, replace the filone loaf ingredients with these ingredients instead and follow the directions for the filone loaf.

OLIVE FILONE

The filone dough is so versatile that it lends itself to a number of variations that create completely different flavor profiles, each wonderful in its own way. My all-time favorite since the opening of Alimentari is the olive loaf. The key is the Castelvetrano olives, green, firm, and sweet with that classic olive bitter tang in the finish. The addition of the olives slightly alters the consistency of the loaf, creating a wonderful chewy texture rich with earthy flavor. These can also be made into smaller batons for a fun on-the-go snack.

Makes 1 loaf

Flour, for dusting
1 batch filone dough (approximately 1,000 grams), made through step 3 of Filone recipe (page 122)
200 grams pitted Castelvetrano olives, roughly chopped

1. Put the dough on a lightly floured surface and let it rest for 20 minutes.

2. Once the dough is rested, sprinkle your olives over the dough and knead by hand until the olives are evenly incorporated throughout the dough. Proceed with proofing, shaping, and baking by following the filone instructions, steps 4 through 9.

SESAME FILONE

The sesame variation lends its own special characteristics. The baked sesame seeds add a nutty, crunchy component that almost caramelizes in the crust to give a wonderful chewy toastiness to this loaf. It's a great sandwich bread or delicious simply dunked in your favorite olive oil with a few flakes of fiore di sale.

Makes 1 loaf

1 batch filone dough, made through creation of the
   boule in step 5 of Filone recipe (page 122)
Flour, for dusting
½ cup unhulled sesame seeds

1. Fill a shallow tray with just enough water to cover the bottom. Put the seeds in a separate tray. Briefly roll the top and sides of the dough into the water bath. Then transfer the wet dough, top side down, to the sesame seed tray, making sure to cover as much of the top and sides as possible. Leave the bottom (the seam side) seedless, as the seeds will burn when baking.

2. Place the dough seam side up in a proofing basket lined with semolina flour to prevent sticking. Sprinkle more semolina over the dough once it is in the basket. Loosely cover with a kitchen towel and refrigerate overnight, anywhere from 12 to 24 hours. Proceed with baking by following the filone loaf instructions, steps 6 through 9.

FOCACCIA

We make three styles of focaccia at il Buco. The first, technically called *pizza bianca*, is ubiquitous in Rome where you will see people with folded pieces of this "white pizza" simply sprinkled with coarse salt and sometimes rosemary, either plain or filled, often with a couple slices of prosciutto or mortadella. That's this focaccia: thin, with puffy air bubbles that make it crunchy and delicious. The second type we call *focaccia fino*, which is made with the very same dough, though we double the recipe, stretch it over a baking sheet, and score it into loaves. We use this at the Alimentari as our delicious sandwich bread. The third is our ancient grain focaccia, more of a technical challenge due to the peculiarities of the ancient grains, but well worth a trip to Ibiza, where it's our staple at Bottega il Buco.

Makes 1 (17-inch) pizza bianca

500 grams all-purpose flour
375 grams warm water (between 78°F and 90°F)
150 grams Sourdough Starter (page 120)
3 grams yeast
10 grams fine sea salt

5 grams granulated sugar
5 tablespoons extra virgin olive oil, divided
¼ teaspoon coarse sea salt
1 sprig rosemary, leaves stripped

Special equipment needed: stand mixer with a dough hook attachment, plastic bowl scraper

1. In the bowl of a stand mixer (or a large bowl if working by hand), place the flour, water, sourdough starter, and yeast. Using the dough hook attachment of the stand mixer, mix at low speed for 5 minutes until a dough forms. Increase the speed to medium and mix for an additional 4 to 5 minutes, until the dough begins to form a satiny finish and begins to pull away from the sides of the bowl. (If mixing by hand, use a bowl scraper to mix until a dough forms, approximately 10 minutes.) Let the dough rest in the bowl, covered with a kitchen towel, for 20 minutes.

2. Meanwhile, in a small bowl, mix together the fine sea salt and sugar. After the dough has rested, sprinkle the salt and sugar mixture over the dough and cut it in using a bowl scraper until well incorporated and you don't feel any granules in the dough.

3. Coat a half sheet pan with 2 tablespoons of olive oil. Form the dough into a round, then add 1 table- spoon olive oil to the top of the dough, spreading it over the entire surface of the dough to prevent it from drying out. Place the dough round on the prepared sheet tray, cover in plastic, and place in the refrigera- tor to proof overnight.

4. Preheat the oven to 450°F. Take the dough out of the refrigerator and let it come to room temperature. Drizzle the dough with 1 tablespoon of the olive oil. Then use your fingers to gently dimple the dough, pressing your fingers down to the bottom of the sheet pan, being careful not to pierce the dough. There should be lots of bubbles, hills, and valleys, and the dough should be relatively even across the round. Drizzle the dimpled dough with the remaining tablespoon of olive oil and sprinkle with the coarse sea salt and rosemary leaves.

5. Place the sheet pan in the middle of the oven. Let bake for 15 minutes, then rotate the pan and continue baking until puffed, golden, and crispy at the edges, about 15 minutes more. Using an offset spatula or a knife, check the bottom of the focaccia; if it's golden brown, then it is ready. Let it cool completely on a cooling rack.

FOCACCIA FINO VARIATION
Makes 3 loaves

Double the ingredients for the focaccia recipe on the opposite page, but keep the olive oil at 5 tablespoons and note that the coarse sea salt and rosemary are optional.

Proceed with steps 1 and 2 in the focaccia recipe, then proceed with the following steps.

Coat a half sheet pan with 2 tablespoons of olive oil. Press the dough into the sheet pan, stretching the dough as close to the sides as possible. Add 1 tablespoon olive oil to the top of the dough, spread- ing it over the entire surface of the dough to prevent it from drying out. Cover the dough with plastic and place in refrigerator to proof overnight. Thirty minutes before baking, remove from refrigerator and bring to room temperature.

Preheat the oven to 450°F. Take the dough out of the refrigerator and let it come to room temperature. Gently stretch the dough to the sides of the sheet pan, taking care not to de-gas the dough. Use your bowl scraper to cut the dough lengthwise into 3 even strips, leaving intact inside the sheet pan. Drizzle with 2 tablespoons of olive oil and sprinkle with coarse sea salt and rosemary if desired. Continue with the baking instructions in step 5 of the focaccia recipe. Let it cool completely on the cooling rack, then separate into 3 loaves.

"We can't count the number of times we've been to il Buco for the infused crudos, perfect porchetta, and housemade bread and olive oil combo that screams scarpetta, connecting us back to Italy..."

—SIMONA VIGNA & ANDREA CALIFANO

BASIC PIZZA DOUGH

When Justin Smillie started offering Roman-style pizza by the slice in 2014, there was a minor riot at the front of Alimentari. Everyone wanted a piece. Since then, we've retired the *a taglio* model because real estate is limited in our wood-fired oven, but we always make sure to have a few options on the menu. Since we opened, New York has become a hotbed of neo-Neapolitan *pizzerie* and we've worked to stay atop our game. While we don't claim to be a purveyor of *vera pizza Napoletana*, we take a lot of pride in our offerings. Sheena, I know, worked for months perfecting the dough so it has just the right amount of elasticity and bite. Preston perfected his *passato,* or sauce. But much of the success is due to the highest quality ingredients—from the San Marzano tomatoes, Scalia anchovies, fresh mozzarella, and Bernardo's lonza—to the scorching heat of the oven. Overall, it's the attention to detail that makes it so good (which is why we weigh ingredients below rather than use volume measures—it's more precise).

Makes enough dough for one 8-inch pizza

190 grams warm water
10 grams, plus 1 tablespoon mild extra virgin olive
    oil (such as Biancolilla), divided
4 grams yeast
280 grams all-purpose flour
10 grams kosher salt

1. Combine the water, 10 grams of the olive oil, and the yeast in the bowl of a stand mixer. Whisk with a fork until the yeast is distributed evenly in the water.

2. Add the flour and salt and mix, using the dough hook attachment at a low speed until the dough becomes a shaggy mass, approximately 2 minutes, or use your hands for approximately 8 to 9 minutes. Scraping down the bowl as necessary, increase speed to medium and mix for an additional 5 to 7 minutes until the dough forms a more coherent mass.

3. Coat a medium-size bowl with 1 tablespoon of olive oil. Remove the dough from the mixing bowl and form into a ball. Place in the oiled bowl. Cover the bowl with plastic wrap and refrigerate overnight until it doubles in size.

4. When ready to form, place a baking stone, if using, in the oven and preheat to 500°F. Allow the dough to come to room temperature.

5. Empty your dough onto a floured surface, keeping the smooth side facing up. Using the pads of your fingers, gently stretch out the dough until the dough is about ¼ inch thick all the way around and about 8 inches in diameter. Be careful to maintain its circular shape.

6. Place the dough onto a parchment paper–lined sheet pan (or floured pizza peel if using a baking stone). Adjust the dough back into a circle if necessary. Top with desired toppings (see pages 130–137).

7. Bake for 15 minutes, until golden on the edges *and* the bottom.

"I've been an il Buco regular since the very beginning. The down-home yet eclectic vibe suits my inner boulevardier. But these days you'll find me at the Alimentari at least twice a month for my pizza fix, the best I've had in my forty-five NYC years. My kind of place indeed…"

—JIM FARMER

ANCHOVY PIZZA

A variation on the classic Margherita pie, this pizza is simplicity itself. I love how the anchovies placed atop at the very end add a burst of salinity that brings me right back to Sicily. As a variation, add torn pieces of zucchini flowers in season for a gorgeous splash of color and a vegetal, textural component.

Serves 2

2 tablespoons extra virgin olive oil
½ white onion, diced
3 garlic cloves, thinly sliced
Sea salt
Freshly ground black pepper
1 teaspoon chopped fresh oregano
1 teaspoon chopped fresh rosemary
1 28-ounce can crushed tomatoes
Flour, for dusting
1 recipe pizza dough, room temperature
    (page 129)
¼ pound fresh mozzarella, roughly torn
    (about ½ cup)
6 to 10 anchovy fillets, packed in olive oil
    (ideally Sicilian or Cantabrian)
⅓ cup torn fresh basil

1. Heat a heavy-bottomed skillet over medium heat. Add the olive oil and heat until it shimmers. Add the onion and garlic, stirring constantly. Season with salt and pepper and cook until the onion turns translucent and the garlic is golden, roughly 10 minutes. Add the oregano and rosemary and then the crushed tomatoes. Bring to a simmer and cook, stirring occasionally, until reduced by one quarter, approximately 10 minutes. Remove from heat, transfer to a bowl, and refrigerate until cooled to room temperature. (The sauce can also be kept refrigerated for 2 days or frozen for 3 months.)

2. Preheat the oven to 500°F. On a lightly floured surface, stretch the pizza dough according to the method on page 129. Place the dough on a lightly floured sheet pan.

3. Using a large spoon, evenly spread ¼ cup of the sauce atop the pizza dough, leaving ¼ inch unsauced around the sides. (Reserve remaining sauce for another use.) Distribute the torn mozzarella evenly across the surface of the pizza.

4. Bake the pizza until the crust is crisp, approximately 15 minutes.

5. Remove the pizza from the oven and immediately top with the anchovies and torn basil leaves. Sprinkle on salt to taste.

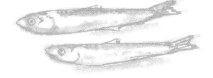

BROCCOLINI PIZZA

Broccoli di cicco, often referred to as baby broccoli or broccolini, has smaller florets and more tender stems than its better known cousin. Though often mistaken for broccoli rabe—which is actually not in the broccoli family at all but part of the turnip family—broccoli di cicco has a lovely sweet flavor. On this pizza, the florets star alongside the gooey stracciatella and the spice of Calabrian chili for a perfect—and healthy—pizza.

Serves 2

Sea salt to taste
1 bunch broccolini, stems trimmed
Flour, for dusting
1 recipe pizza dough, room temperature
   (page 129)
¼ pound fresh stracciatella
½ teaspoon thinly sliced Calabrian chili
½ tablespoon extra virgin olive oil
Freshly cracked black pepper to taste

1. Preheat the oven to 500°F.

2. Bring a pot of salted water to boil over high heat. Prepare an ice bath: fill a medium bowl with ice and cold water and set aside.

3. Once the water reaches a boil, add the broccolini and blanch until it turns a vibrant green and you can pierce the stems easily with a paring knife, 3 to 4 minutes. Remove the broccolini and plunge in the ice bath. Drain, pat dry, roughly chop, and set aside.

4. On a lightly floured surface, stretch the pizza dough according to the method on page 129. Place the dough on a lightly floured sheet pan.

5. Tear the stracciatella into small pieces by hand and sprinkle evenly over the pizza, then sprinkle broccolini on top. Finish with the sliced chilis and a swirl of olive oil, and season with salt and pepper.

6. Cook the pizza until the crust turns golden brown, approximately 15 minutes.

7. Remove the pizza from the oven. Serve immediately.

BREAKFAST PIZZA

Since we introduced it at brunch, this has been a favorite at Alimentari. That's no surprise because it is basically a breakfast sandwich in pizza form. It's decadent and comforting, exactly what you want during a long leisurely brunch with friends. Bernardo's cured lonza, made from pork loin, adds just the right touch of saltiness, much healthier than any greasy bacon alternative.

....

Serves 2

1 cup cherry tomatoes
1 tablespoon extra virgin olive oil
Fine sea salt
Freshly ground black pepper
Flour, for dusting
1 recipe pizza dough, room temperature
    (page 129)
¼ pound fresh mozzarella, roughly torn
    (about ½ cup)
2 eggs
1 tablespoon chopped oregano
⅛ pound lonza, sliced (approximately 8 slices)
Small handful of arugula

"Il Buco is one of the reasons New York is still such a special place."

—DENISE PORCARO

1. Preheat the oven to 500°F.

2. Place the cherry tomatoes on a small rimmed sheet pan. Toss with the olive oil and season generously with salt and pepper. Roast for about 8 minutes, until the tomatoes start to burst but are not yet brown. Scrape the tomatoes and any oil onto a plate and transfer them, uncovered, to the refrigerator to cool.

3. On a lightly floured surface, shape the pizza dough into an 8-inch round, according to the method on page 129.

4. Top the dough with cooled cherry tomatoes, liquid and all. Scatter the mozzarella evenly on top. Leave two uncovered spots toward the center of the pizza to crack the eggs into later.

5. Bake the pizza for 8 minutes, until the crust starts to brown around the edges and the cheese melts. Remove the pizza from the oven and crack the eggs into the two uncovered spaces. Return to the oven and bake an additional 7 minutes, until the crust is golden brown and the whites of the eggs are set but the yolks are runny.

6. Sprinkle on the oregano. Drape the lonza atop the pie and top with arugula. Slice (avoid bursting the egg yolks) and serve immediately.

ANCHOVY & BUTTER CROSTINI

This simple crostino is about as unlikely a combination of ingredients as you'll find. Dairy and seafood rarely play well together, but the deliciousness of these flavors is indisputable: preserved anchovies from the eastern coast of Sicily procured from our dear friend Baldo Scalia, and freshly made butter atop a crisp tranche of buckwheat rye blend cream, brine, and the dense nuttiness of the bread. All across Italy, this crostino, also called *burro e alici*, is a beloved antipasto. In fact, in Rome, where it enjoys particular adoration, if you want to say something has gone well, you can say that it went "a burro e alici." When guests come to my beach house in East Hampton, I always like to have a plate of burro e alici awaiting them. I have to admit, I don't often make my own butter, but Sheena does, and it makes all the difference. Instead I focus on the proportions: the most important thing for me is to use enough of the butter that you can see it spread beneath the anchovies but not so much that you get a mouth full of it.

Serves 4

1 quart heavy cream
1 cup buttermilk
⅛ teaspoon fine sea salt
4 thick slices buckwheat rye bread (page 123)
20 anchovy fillets, packed in olive oil
    (approximately 1 tin, preferably Sicilian
    or Cantabrian)

"That little hole in the wall is unbelievable!"
—JOSEPH LAUTO

1. Prepare the butter by mixing together the cream and buttermilk in a nonreactive container. Let sit at room temperature overnight until thick.

2. Using a whisk attachment in a mixer, beat the mixture at medium speed until it breaks into curds (solids) and whey (liquid).

3. Pour the mixture slowly through a cheesecloth, allowing the whey to flow into a bowl. Knead the curds to force out as much whey as possible.

4. Add salt to the curds and knead again. Transfer the solids into a nonreactive container and let chill, covered, overnight.

5. To serve, grill or toast the buckwheat rye for a little color. Cut the toasts into halves or thirds. Spread a good amount of butter on each piece. (You want the butter to be a visible layer.) Then, equally divide the anchovies and layer atop the butter. Serve immediately.

SPICY CALAMARI CROSTINI

Nowadays, the interchange between *bruschette* (singular *bruschetta*)—a grilled slice of bread simply rubbed with garlic and slathered with olive oil, or piled high with chopped tomatoes and basil—and *crostini*, literally "little crusts," has blurred beyond recognition. Today any seasonal ingredient, thrown on a great slice of crusty grilled or toasted bread served along a glass of well paired wine, will bring an instant smile. This combination, first brought to the Alimenari by sous chef Carlo Biggi, is a showstopper. The tender calamari, perfectly seared and tossed with roasted cherry tomatoes and a dose of Calabrian chili, is the last thing you might expect on a grilled slice of bread, but I assure you, with the built-in "scarpetta," it's a little bit of heaven on toast. Be sure to give the bread a strong toast to hold up to the juices!

Serves 4

1 tablespoon extra virgin olive oil
¼ pound calamari, including tentacles, cleaned, tubes sliced into ⅓-inch rounds (about ¾ cup)
Fine sea salt to taste
Freshly ground black pepper
2 garlic cloves, thinly sliced
1 pint cherry tomatoes (ideally Sungolds)
1 peperoncino, crumbled, or to taste
1 tablespoon lemon juice
1 tablespoon chopped parsley
4 slices filone bread (page 122), ¾ inch thick, well toasted

1. Add the olive oil to a large cast iron skillet over high heat. Once the oil is shimmering, add the calamari and sear. Season with salt and pepper and cook, without stirring, for 1 to 2 minutes, until the calamari is sizzling and just beginning to firm up.

2. Add the garlic and stir for 30 seconds. Add the cherry tomatoes and crumbled peperoncino and cook, stirring often until the liquids reduce and thicken, 3 to 4 minutes. Remove the pan from the heat and stir in the lemon juice and parsley.

3. Heap 2 tablespoons of the calamari mixture atop each slice of toast, sprinkle with salt, cut each piece of toast in half, and serve immediately.

CHANTARELLE & RICOTTA CROSTINI

Since day one, we've been making our own ricotta in-house, in part to avoid paying for something that is so simple and easy to do yourself, but mostly because why settle for a ricotta that isn't achingly fresh? The side effect of this is we're always looking for ways to utilize and enjoy it. We stuff it in zucchini flowers in the summer (page 34), pair it with sugar snaps in the spring (page 58), and fry it into crisp fritters in the fall. Another beautiful fall preparation is to pair this milky cheese with the crisp woodsy chanterelle, a delicious mushroom that is widely available in late summer. As for the crispy sage on top, here it adds a particularly fine textural note with the golden brown and delicious mushrooms.

Serves 4

½ cup plus 2 tablespoons olive oil, divided, plus
    more for finishing
16 sage leaves, plus 1 tablespoon chopped
4 slices filone bread (page 122), ½ inch thick
8 ounces chanterelle mushrooms, cleaned and
    bottoms trimmed
Sea salt to taste
Freshly ground black pepper to taste
1 small shallot, sliced thinly
4 sprigs thyme, leaves chopped
1 cup fresh ricotta (page 58)

1. Add ½ cup of the olive oil to a frying pan (it should be about ½ inch deep) and heat to 375°F. Add four sage leaves at a time and fry until crisp, approximately 5 seconds. Remove the leaves with a slotted spoon and drain on a paper towel; repeat with the remaining leaves.

2. Grill or toast the filone bread until slightly browned. Set aside.

3. Heat the remaining 2 tablespoons of olive oil in a large skillet over medium heat until shimmering. Add the chanterelle mushrooms to the skillet and season with salt and pepper. After a few minutes, once the chanterelles becomes crisp on the edges, add the shallot, chopped sage, and thyme. Sauté the shallot, herbs, and mushrooms for 3 to 4 minutes, until golden brown.

4. Spread the ricotta evenly on the bread. Equally divide the mushrooms and then the sage leaves on top. Finish with a drizzle of olive oil and sea salt, cut each piece of toast in half, and serve immediately.

IL SALE

———

Finally making landfall after a long journey across the Mediterranean, the hot wind ripples across the surface of the fields of water around me. I'm standing on the edge of this ancient magical salina, *or salt pan, embraced by its beauty. Here in Trapani, on the northwestern coast of Sicily, the world distills itself into primary colors and shapes. Blindingly white pyramids of coarse salt crystals; the vast blue sky; the perfect circle of the September sun, so bright and close I feel like I could reach out and touch it.*

Around me stand a half-dozen *salinai*, or salt harvesters, burly men, some clutching a small shovel called *u paluneddro* and others holding the wooden handles of battered wheelbarrows laden with crystals. Some are just teenagers from the neighboring towns. Some are old men who have spent their lives carting salt back and forth. Either way, their skin is tanned like leather, their muscles ripple under flimsy tank tops, and their high rubber boots are caked with salt. They work standing atop the salt like the Phoenicians did a millennium ago. Salt. Sky. Sun. Wind. Life pulses here, as shimmering and rich

as the heat waves distorting the windmills and the horizon in the distance.

Salt is the most elemental of all seasonings. To even call it a seasoning is to sell salt short. Salt gives muscle to flavor. Salt preserves. Salt sustains. We need sodium to live. Salt is so valuable in society it is the root of the word *salary* (literally "salt money") and so essential in the kitchen it is also the root of the word *sauce*. In the kitchen, salt is as necessary to a chef as perspective is to a painter. Without it, everything is flat. And yet, for so important and integral an ingredient—and perhaps because it is so omni-

LEFT: Salt harvest, Salina Galia, Trapani, Italy

present on our tables—people rarely think of salt as anything but a health menace, at best, a shaker full of inert matter in the center of the table.

My journey into the world of salt started in Trapani, a speck of a town on the far west coast of Sicily, 100 kilometers west of Palermo and 30 kilometers short of Marsala (a province of Trapani). I first visited the area in 1999 in the company of Alberto, whose view of salt rested between veneration and obsession. Alberto held salt in the same reverence in which he held olive oil, balsamic vinegar, bread, wine, everything sensual, really. When speaking about salt he was prone to break into poetry. Actual poetry, like the line from Pablo Neruda's "Ode to Salt":

> Dust of the sea, in you
> the tongue receives a kiss
> from ocean night:
> taste imparts to every seasoned
> dish your ocean essence;
> the smallest,
> miniature
> wave from the saltcellar
> reveals to us
> more than domestic whiteness;
> in it, we taste infinitude.

He had brought me to this coastal marshland so rich with wildlife that nearly 2,000 hectares of it are a nature marine preserve, because it has been the center of Italy's salt trade for the last 2,700 years. France has Guerande; the Brits have Maldon; Italy has Trapani.

When we arrived that summer, in the late '90s, he whisked me off to the island of Mozia, a little strip of land just off the coast between Trapani and Marsala, where Antonio Dali had created an almost fairy-tale setting in which to discover the craft of salt making. Huge antique windmills still dotted the shoreline, one serving as a museum to salt, with a lineup of passenger boats carting tourists back and forth to Mozia island, where a full homage to the history of salt was presented in another well-curated museum. We did the tour on that first voyage, but Alberto had already met the owner, Dali, and his right-hand man, Salvatore Daidone, and was already consumed with making a business deal and acquiring the prestigious *fiore di sale*, or "flower of salt," for il Buco. Thus began our first salt import. As time went on, Salvatore became our trusted contact, and as Sicilian life would have it, struggles with Dali's son would lead Salvatore to seek his own place "in the sun."

Having worked in *saline* all his life, Salvatore Daidone, the *curatolo*, or "shepherd," of the Salina di Trapani, an extremely affable forty-year-old, decided to restore the once famous Galia salt pan, where his own father had harvested, and which had been left fallow. As Salvatore walked us along a narrow raised pathway of dried bricks called *tufa* at the edge of the salt pans, we passed brilliant purple clumps of sea lavender and tendrils of sea blite. At the edge of the vast salt pans, areas larger than a football field, the water's surface shimmered endlessly in the changing light. Glinting silver, blinding white, pinks and corals, incandescent blue, the sky's hues came alive in the earth in the reflections on the water's surface. At dusk, the colors shift from delicate pastels—robin's-egg blue, pale pink, gentle orange—to brilliant Technicolor, almost psychedelic displays, mirroring the setting sun. Flocks of flamingos, long-limbed egrets, and avocets with their small curved beaks, streaked across the crimson sky, headed north from Africa.

As Salvatore explained, the task of the curatolo was to orchestrate the movement of water through the series of *vasche*, or pans, that begin with those closest to the sea. As the waters flow into them over the course of forty to ninety days, the water naturally, gently evaporates, leaving the liquid more and more saturated with salt crystals. The first *vasca*, called *fridde* in Sicilian dialect, is pure seawater. But as the water moves next to the *frisca*, then to the *caure*, to the *sentina*, the water evaporates. By the time the water

enters the *casaddre*, the final salt pan, the relentless sun and crushing heat have evaporated nearly all the water, leaving snowy white granules of salt that rest like a layer of wet snow in the pan. Because the process has occurred naturally—as opposed to by aggressive heating through mechanical means—these crystals maintain the highest level of nutrients and trace minerals. Like so much of what we love at il Buco, salt takes time and patience.

There are many other ways to make salt, of course, and even in Trapani, various saline have modernized the process. Today big monopolies like SoSalt churn out salt for industrial use as well as culinary, roads as well as salads. But Salvatore was passionate about preserving the methods of the past. His philosophy was ours too: do the least possible to the best possible product. In Trapani, he had found the cradle of salt, and in him, we had found a kindred spirit.

People rarely think of salt being seasonal but, as they say, to everything there is a season, and salt season occurs between July and September. During the harvest, teams of husky men seize their *paluneddu* and head into the salt pans at dawn. Meter after meter, through the salt pan they work, shoveling the now mostly dry crystals into neat small pyramids that dot the pan at regular intervals. These they load up into wheelbarrows and consolidate near the water's edge into massively high pyramids called *arioni*. These are eventually covered in terra-cotta roofing tiles to protect the salt as the liquid drains from these hills. At the end of the season the salt is milled into either *fino* (fine) or *grosso* (coarse) grains.

Seeing these arioni, meeting Salvatore, being in Trapani, was a revelation to me, much like walking with Marco Pandolfi through his olive trees in Umbria. My eyes opened to the possibilities of salt. It was as if I had found the key to something, or been let in on a secret that was before me the entire time. It is the secret that transforms your food.

Almost immediately we began to import Salvatore's salt, both the large crystals, called the sale grosso, and a finer form, the sale fino. The only difference between the two was how much he milled the crystals after the harvest. We used the salt both in the kitchen and at the table. Sara Jenkins, our chef at the time, loved how potent it was. Just a pinch of sea salt could do the work of a steady pour of table salt. Used as a finishing condiment on everything from salads to crudo, the muscular crystals and delicate flakes popped in the mouth, releasing a surprisingly complex burst of flavor.

When clients sat down at il Buco, we offered them a few thick slices of freshly made bread, a cruet of Umbrian olive oil, and a ramekin of Trapanese salt. Salvatore's salt was a revelation. Taken together, this trio formed the underpinnings of what was to come: a simple meal, made extraordinary by the quality of the ingredients and the work required to harvest them.

What we call table salt, like processed sugar or white bread, is optimized for the shelf, not the palate. With crystals formed by mechanical compression, it dissolves almost instantaneously, so more salt is needed to obtain the same flavor. Not only that, many common salts contain a host of anticaking chemicals like calcium silicate, and even more chemicals to prevent *those* from clumping. These added chemicals have given salt such a negative rap.

Alberto, as usual, wanted to go further, go finer. After years of our trying to convince him, Salvatore finally agreed to start producing the crème de la crème, the fiore di sale. Known in French as *fleur de sel*, fiore di sale is the most labor intensive, rare, and prized of all salts. Like a vintage champagne, it forms only periodically, when the mix of meteorological conditions, including low wind and low humidity, allow a crystalline skein to form spontaneously in the salt pan. This layer, as translucent and delicate as a sheet of mica, is carefully harvested with wooden shovels across the surface of the salina and dropped into wooden baskets at the edge of it. It is the most sublime expression of the salt. Untouched by any machinery, it maintains the highest levels of magne-

CLOCKWISE FROM TOP LEFT: Donna and Alberto, Trapani, Sicily; Scala dei Turchi ("Turkish Steps"), Agrigento, Sicily; Sicilian happy couple; tufa path to windmills, Salina Galia; salina detail; Joaquin; salina landscape

sium and potassium as well as more than ninety trace minerals. Harvesting fiore di sale is a difficult, unpredictable, and expensive endeavor, one reason why so few Trapanese saline produce it. But Alberto was peristent. He would leave no flower unpicked. With our support—moral and financial—Salvatore began to harvest fiore di sale exclusively for il Buco.

For the next ten years, our relationship with Salvatore continued to deepen. And just as had happened with Marco and many other producers, Salvatore became part of the il Buco family and, therefore, part of my family as well. When Joaquin was two years old, I brought him to the salina. I still remember him seated on Salvatore's lap pretending to drive through the salt pans or gingerly climbing the steps of the old windmill, converted into the office for the salina.

We went on numerous trips with Salvatore on his motorboat across the Trapanese channel to the beautiful islands of Favignana and Marettimo. During one visit in September 2001, returning from a trip to Umbria for Marco Pandolfi's wedding, we were lunching with Salvatore when we received the news of the downing of the twin towers in NYC. Together with Salvatore, we huddled in front of the restaurant's television, following the tragic day's events.

It was another tragic day in 2006, when olive oil producer Alberto Gallufo, our mutual friend, called to tell us Salvatore was battling liver cancer. During his illness, we spoke regularly. When he traveled to Texas for his treatments, he would come to see us in New York. Sadly, he passed away in 2009.

To compound the sadness, after Salvatore's passing, the future of the salina was thrown into chaos and uncertainty. Sicily being Sicily, there was a tussle for the land and the management of the salina. There were internecine squabbles, a bank stepped in, and the pans grew dry. For a few years, it looked like the salina would return to being unused. But eventually, Massimo Daidone, Salvatore's distant relative, who had worked with Salvatore in the salina for years, stepped in to take over.

He and his wife, Alberta, put everything they owned into bringing the salina back to life.

Like Salvatore, Massimo is an arch-traditionalist when it comes to salt. In fact, he wanted to go even further than Salvatore. Inspired by the methods of the Phoenicians who manufactured salt on the very same salt pans a millennium ago, last year Massimo hired some local artisans to construct a completely manual mill, eliminating the need for any heat to crush the natural crystals. The result is the purest salt. Now the salt arrives on Bond Street still wet, laden with the unevaporated saltwater from half a world away.

In 2016 I took my nephew, Danny, with me on a two-week trip through Italy. An avid fisherman, consummate foodie, and great cook in his own right, Danny was a tremendous asset and soaked up every detail. He met all of our producers throughout Umbria, the Marche, and Sicily, but the experience in Trapani was transformative. After a tour of the salina, watching the *operai* at work, Massimo and Alberta put out a beautiful picnic lunch at a long wooden table in front of the ancient windmill/office. We feasted on the most simply delicious local vegetables marinated in olive oil, home-baked semolina bread, local cheeses, olives, and assorted delicacies as the sun slowly sank beneath the horizon and the colors danced off the water.

Danny returned to New York to head up the Alimentari and became the liaison with Alberto and all our producers. In our work together with Massimo, our salt has become more and more elemental. Danny, Alberto, and Massimo race each other to see how close to the earth they can go. The latest project regards the production of *acqua madri*, the liquid residue naturally drained from the hills of salt. Once filtered, this liquid represents the purest, most powerful expression of nutrients derived from salt, loaded with magnesium, potassium, and trace minerals much like the pure fiore di sale. The Japanese call it *nigari* and many drink a teaspoon a day. Alberto does too and he will tell you it's the closest thing to mother's milk. It's a literal drop of Trapani brought to the heart of New York.

RIGHT: Freshly harvested salt crystals FOLLOWING: Sea and tufa bricks, Trapani

ZUPPE E INSALATE

GAZPACHO A LA ANDALUZ

Gazpacho is essentially a liquified summer salad, one that Alberto fell in love with while living in Spain. Soothing, spicy, and cool, gazpacho a la Andaluz is traditionally served at the end of the meal on a hot summer day, and it was the only soup on our opening menu. Over years of making it at home, Alberto modified the dish to his taste. The grapes and bread are traditional, the apple isn't. And then there's the kick: Alberto always loved heat, provided here by the peperoncino. Although this is our take on this dish, the underlying appeal of gazpacho—something to soothe you, something to excite you, something to etch summer into your mind—remains.

Serves 4

1 (1-inch) slice day-old filone (page 122)
    or country bread
2 pounds ripe tomatoes (4 medium),
    seeded and chopped
2 cucumbers, peeled, seeded, and chopped
½ white onion, chopped
2 orange and/or yellow bell peppers,
    seeded and chopped
1 jalapeño pepper, seeded and chopped
1 semisweet apple (such as Honeycrisp),
    chopped but not peeled
2 garlic cloves, chopped
2 sprigs basil, plus more for garnish
1 peperoncino, crumbled, or to taste
½ cup extra virgin olive oil, divided,
    plus more for garnish
2 tablespoons white balsamic vinegar
1 teaspoon kosher salt
12 seedless grapes, halved, for garnish

1. In a bowl, place the bread, tomatoes, cucumbers, onion, peppers, apple, garlic, basil, and crumbled peperoncino. Dress with ¼ cup of olive oil, the vinegar, and salt.

2. Transfer the vegetable mixture into a food processor and blend together until all the vegetables are broken down. Add the remaining ¼ cup of olive oil while blending to create emulsification. Texture should be smooth and thick. Cover and refrigerate for at least 2 hours or overnight.

3. To serve, ladle the cold soup into bowls and garnish with halved grapes, a sprig of basil, and a drizzle of olive oil.

"I have so many fond memories of the last 25 years: Roberto's big smile upon passing through the velvet curtains, sharing late-night dinners in the wine cellar with friends, or drinking our sherries in 'The Cask of Amontillado' cellar, bringing back memories of Andalucia."

—ANDRÉ TAMERS

PAPPA AL POMODORO

If you've never heard Italian pop star Rita Pavone's classic 1960s hit "Viva la pappa col pomodoro," I suggest you don't, because it will get stuck in your head forever. I do, however, recommend you try the *pappa al pomodoro* itself. A classic Tuscan dish of ancient origin, the thick bread soup is basically a problem solver: what do you do with all this stale bread and all these lovely tomatoes? In Spain, the answer is gazpacho. In Italy, the answer is pappa al pomodoro, a super simple but delicious dish, half sauce, half soup. In its most classic form, pappa is made solely with crusty bread, tomato, salt, and olive oil, but, as with so many classic recipes, this one tolerates variation, in this case, the addition of garlic, onion, basil, and a hint of chili for heat. It's the most soothing dish on the planet.

Serves 4

3 to 4 slices filone or country bread, torn into
    ½-inch chunks
4 pounds ripe beefsteak tomatoes (about 8 large)
½ cup plus 1 tablespoon extra virgin olive oil, divided
½ white onion, diced
3 garlic cloves, minced
½ teaspoon sea salt, plus additional for finishing
1 peperoncino (optional)
3 tablespoons finely chopped basil, plus more sprigs
    for garnish

1. Preheat the oven to 350°F. Spread the bread on a sheet pan, drizzle with 2 tablespoons of olive oil, and toast approximately 10 minutes.

2. Meanwhile, prepare the tomatoes by cutting an X in the top of each using a paring knife. Bring a large pot of salted water to boil and prepare an ice bath by filling a medium-size bowl with ice and cold water and set aside.

3. Once the water is boiling, add the tomatoes for between 45 seconds and 1 minute. Remove and plunge into the ice bath. Once the tomatoes are cool enough to handle, peel off the skin (it should come off easily). Core and crush the tomatoes, doing so over an empty bowl to reserve the juice.

4. In a large skillet over medium heat, heat ½ cup olive oil until shimmering. Add the onion and garlic, lowering the heat to medium-low and allowing to cook until the onions are translucent and the garlic soft, 4 to 5 minutes. Add the crushed tomatoes and bring to a simmer over medium heat, whisking to break up large chunks of tomato. Do not let the tomatoes boil. Allow the liquid to reduce. The pappa should be the consistency of a thick soup.

5. Add salt and peperoncino if desired, stirring the mixture gently. Remove from heat and add torn-up bread to the skillet, stirring to break up and coat the bread. Let the bread and soup mixture sit for 30 minutes so the bread is incorporated into the tomato. If it is too thick, strain the reserved tomato juice, discarding seeds, and add.

6. Stir in the chopped basil and another tablespoon of extra virgin olive oil.

7. Serve at room temperature, dividing equally among four bowls and garnishing with basil sprigs.

UMBRIAN CHICKPEA SOUP

When fall arrives and the il Buco kitchen starts turning out the legume soups, fragrant with chicken broth and Parmigiano-Reggiano, my appetite comes to life. Throw in some fresh veggies, wilted spinach, and those wonderful Umbrian *ceci*, or chickpeas, and that's all I need to turn my day around. We have been importing our beans and legumes from Umbria for many years, working with wonderful producers like Cuore Verde and our friends the Marini brothers. The village of Castellucio is the top spot for lentil and ceci production, and a visit to that glorious plateau, paragliders coloring the sky, surrounded by poppy and ceci fields after a long windy travel through Norcia, reminds me why it is one of Umbria's hidden gems.

Serves 4

For the chicken stock
½ pound raw chicken bones
1 small carrot, peeled and roughly chopped
2 celery ribs, trimmed and roughly chopped
1 large white onion, peeled and quartered
1½ teaspoons black peppercorns
1 bay leaf

For the soup
½ cup dried chickpeas, preferably Umbrian, soaked
    overnight in cold water, then drained
1 white onion, peeled and halved
1 carrot, peeled and halved
2 garlic cloves
1 bay leaf
½ teaspoon sea salt, plus more to taste
3 tablespoons extra virgin olive oil
1 stalk celery, finely diced
2 sprigs thyme, leaves removed
½ teaspoon chopped sage leaves
2 cups spinach
Freshly ground black pepper
Juice of ½ lemon
2 tablespoons chopped parsley
¼ cup shaved Parmigiano-Reggiano

1. To make the stock, preheat the oven to 350°F.

2. Arrange the bones in large roasting pan and roast until evenly browned, about 30 to 45 minutes.

3. Transfer pan contents to a stockpot. Add the carrot, celery, onion, peppercorns, bay leaf, and cover with water. Bring to a boil, then lower to a gentle simmer and cook for 2 hours, skimming off any fat or froth. Strain the stock over a bowl and discard the solids.

4. For the soup, place the chickpeas in a large saucepan with one half of the onion, one half of the carrot, the garlic cloves, and the bay leaf. Add ½ teaspoon sea salt and enough water to cover, and bring to a boil over high heat. Lower to a simmer and let cook up to an hour, adding more water as needed to keep the chickpeas submerged, until they are tender. Drain, reserving the chickpea water, and discard the vegetables.

5. Meanwhile, finely dice the remaining onion and carrot halves. Heat 2 tablespoons olive oil in a large sauté pan over medium heat until shimmering. Add the diced onion, carrot, and celery and sauté, stirring constantly, until soft, about 4 to 5 minutes.

6. Drizzle in the remaining olive oil, the reserved chickpea liquid, and approximately 1 quart of the chicken stock. Add the chickpeas, thyme leaves, sage, and salt to taste. Bring to a boil, then simmer for 15 minutes. Add the spinach and cook, stirring occasionally, until wilted, 3 to 4 minutes more.

7. To serve, season with sea salt, black pepper, and lemon juice. Garnish with chopped parsley and a few wide shavings of Parmigiano-Reggiano.

KALE SALAD

This salad arrived with Ignacio Mattos in the spring of 2005. We had been looking for a new chef for several months. One day, while I was visiting Francis Mallmann at his home in East Quogue, he suggested a young guy named Ignacio, who worked with him in Uruguay. "He's a little hot-headed," he warned, "but super talented." *Okay*, I thought, *hot-headed I can handle.*

Ignacio, affectionately known as Nacho, flew up for a tasting shortly thereafter. He made a squash polenta with crispy sage that melted in my mouth. It was simple but delicious, instinctive. This, I would learn, was Nacho's genius. The recipe is his version of Judy Rogers's famous caesar salad from San Francisco's Zuni Café. Instead of the standard romaine, we use Tuscan kale, which has a bit more body and character. The greens are great, but the croutons are divine, golden chunks of filone bread that are tossed in the dressing.

Ignacio's arrival coincided with the birth of Joaquin, and I used to eat this protein-filled, iron-rich salad every day while I was breastfeeding him. Amazingly, I never got tired of it and neither have our customers. His salad remains one of the most popular things on the menu for our customers, for me, and, happily, for Joaquin too.

Serves 4 to 6

6 anchovy fillets, packed in olive oil, minced

3 garlic cloves, finely minced

1½ cups plus 2 tablespoons extra virgin olive oil, divided

1 tablespoon red wine vinegar

1 large egg yolk

1 to 2 lemons

4 (1-inch) slices day-old filone bread, torn into 1½-inch chunks

Fine sea salt to taste

2 bunches (about 2 pounds) Tuscan black kale, stems discarded, leaves torn, rinsed and dried

3 ounces freshly grated Parmigiano-Reggiano, plus more for garnish

Freshly ground black pepper to taste

1. Place the anchovies and garlic in a mortar and pestle and blend together. Set aside.

2. In a bowl, whisk together ½ cup of the olive oil, the vinegar, and egg yolk. Stir in the anchovy mixture. Slowly drizzle 1 cup olive oil into the egg mixture, whisking continuously to form an emulsion. Whisk in the juice of 1 lemon; add additional lemon to taste.

3. Preheat the oven to 350°F.

4. Place the bread on a sheet pan. Toss the pieces with the remaining 2 tablespoons of olive oil and sprinkle with salt. Toast on the middle rack of the oven until golden, approximately 15 minutes.

5. To assemble, add the croutons to a large bowl and toss with half the vinaigrette. Add kale, the rest of vinaigrette, a squeeze of lemon, Parmigiano-Reggiano, and salt to taste. Toss well and serve, topping with additional Parmigiano-Reggiano and black pepper to taste.

"I think il Buco invented the kale salad that went on to take over the world."

—MAGGIE GYLLENHAAL

FAVA BEANS, PECORINO & MINT

Fava beans are hardy legumes, one reason they're often used as a cover crop. During fava bean season in early spring, you'll find fava beans all over Umbria. Fresh fava beans and pecorino are an unbeatable combination. The pungent cheese plays delightfully to the fresh vegetal sweetness of the beans. In Italy, the fava beans are often thrown on a wooden board still inside their large unruly pods, with chunks of pecorino on the side—the guests must do the work themselves, shucking these pods to bring forth first the skin-covered bean, and then the tender fruit inside. The shucking of the beans is indeed laborious. But, ultimately, worth the work.

In this case, the work of the fava bean is done in the back as we do for our guests at the restaurant. The tender shucked beans are tossed with shards of this sharp pecorino, and in our version, we accentuate the dynamic with a touch of mint and a pop of citrus.

Serves 4

2 pounds shelled fava beans, fresh or frozen (or
approximately 8 pounds unshelled fava beans)*
4 ounces pecorino toscano, crumbled into fine
shards
3 tablespoons extra virgin olive oil
1 teaspoon sea salt
1 tablespoon lemon juice
1 cup torn fresh mint leaves
Freshly ground black pepper

The larger the fava bean gets (i.e., later in the season), the starchier it becomes. So be sure you're picking your fava beans early and small and eating them early and often.

1. If using whole fava beans, shell the beans and discard the pods. Bring a medium-size pot of salted water to a boil. In the meantime, prepare an ice bath by filling a large bowl with ice cubes and cold water. Once the water is boiling, add the beans to the pot. Blanch the beans for 20 to 30 seconds. Using a small colander or slotted spoon, quickly remove the beans from the boiling water and plunge them into the ice bath. Scoop the beans out of the ice bath and spread them on a towel to drain. Gently peel off the outer casings to expose the tender beans inside. Place the beans in a medium-size bowl and discard the casings.

2. Add the pecorino shards, olive oil, sea salt, lemon juice, and most of the mint to the beans and gently toss to combine.

3. To serve, arrange the fava beans on four small plates, top with a few mint leaves and a generous turn of black pepper.

PUNTARELLE SALAD

Puntarelle is a type of chicory, originally from Catalonia but found widely in Italy. It is intensely crunchy with a lovely balance of bitter and sweet. A head of puntarelle looks almost punky, with dark green spearlike tips. (*Puntarelle* means "little points" in Italian.) Though you can use the darker green leaves, the stalks are more commonly used in Roman cuisine.

The traditional rendition pairs it with an anchovy dressing, which is how we do at il Buco. The garlicky, salty fishiness adds a third dimension to the bitter sweetness of the puntarelle. My favorite thing about this salad, though, is how it looks: like a crunchy little nest. How amazing, I always think, that nature created something so stunning.

Serves 4

2 small heads puntarelle
8 to 10 anchovy fillets, packed in olive oil
3 garlic cloves
½ cup red wine vinegar
Juice and zest of 1 lemon
1 cup extra virgin olive oil
⅛ teaspoon chili flakes (optional)
Fine sea salt to taste

1. Remove the dark outer leaves from the heads of the puntarelle and reserve for soup or pasta. Using a paring knife, cut each stalk away from the base of the plant. Some of the interior smaller stalks will be more fused together, so separate them lengthwise. Julienne the puntarelle lengthwise but leave the smaller bulbs whole, as they add a wonderful crunch. While making the dressing, place the cut puntarelle into ice water for about 30 minutes to become wonderfully crisp and curly.

2. Pound the anchovies and the garlic in a mortar and pestle until a rough paste forms. Transfer the paste to a nonreactive bowl and whisk in the vinegar and lemon, then the olive oil in a slow stream until emulsified. Add lemon zest and chili flakes, if desired, and a pinch of salt.

3. To serve, drain and thoroughly pat or spin dry the puntarelle. (It must be completely dry so the dressing adheres to the leaves.) Toss the puntarelle with the dressing and serve immediately.

PANZANELLA

Il Bacco Felice, "the happy bacchus," was my friend Salvatore Denaro's restaurant in Foligno. It was here that Roberto began his career in wine, assisting Salvatore in exploring the fruits of the vine. Was it a restaurant? Not exactly. It was more like an extension of Salvatore's soul, open to the public and mixed with his *orto*, or herb garden. He almost didn't cook; he assembled nature on the plate. I don't think he'd ever seen a measuring cup in his life. This was perhaps most evident in his tran- scendent panzanella, a traditional summer salad that combines fresh tomatoes, day-old bread, and whatever vegetables you have in your garden into a tangy-sweet salad. As Alberto and I waited with our bottle of wine, Salvatore would duck into his kitchen garden and return a few minutes later, arms full of the juiciest tomatoes I'd ever seen. He'd disappear into the kitchen for another few minutes and then return, bearing the panzanella, another bottle, a ball of fresh mozzarella, and a huge smile.

Serves 4

4 slices day-old filone bread (page 122), torn into 1½- to 2-inch pieces (about 4 cups)

2 tablespoons plus ½ cup extra virgin olive oil, divided

4 large heirloom tomatoes, various colors, quartered

1 pint mixed cherry tomatoes, halved

2 Persian cucumbers, thickly sliced

½ red onion, thinly sliced

¼ cup red wine vinegar

1 garlic clove, minced

1 teaspoon sea salt

2 sprigs green basil, leaves roughly chopped (about 2 tablespoons), plus more for garnish

1 sprig purple basil, leaves roughly chopped (about 1 tablespoon), plus more for garnish

1. Preheat the oven to 350°F. Drizzle the bread with 2 tablespoons of olive oil and spread on a baking sheet. Transfer to the oven and toast until the bread is crusty at the edges and golden, 5 to 7 minutes. Set aside.

2. Meanwhile, combine the tomatoes, cucumbers, and onion in a large bowl. Toss with the remaining ½ cup olive oil and the vinegar, garlic, and salt.

3. Add the toasted bread and the chopped green and purple basil. Gently toss to coat but take care not to crush the tomatoes.

4. Let the salad marinate for 15 to 20 minutes before serving, so the bread absorbs all the juices. Garnish with a few more sprigs of green and purple basil.

"Il Buco is our second kitchen. Donna did something so special with this nook in New York City…there's fairy dust sprinkled over the doorway."

—LESLIE BIBB

L'ACETO

———

Up a steep winding pass in the foothills of the Apennine Mountains stands the house of Sante Bertoni and his balsamic vinegar workshop, the Acetaia Delizia Estense. Although Sante passed away a few years ago, I still half expect him to greet me at the kitchen door as he had in the years past when we visited, a bottle of lambrusco in his hand and a glass ready for filling in the other.

Sante was a dog lover, and the bays of his fifteen English pointers still greet us, their sleek bodies quivering with excitement as we crunch down the gravel driveway to the estate and step out of the van to greet them in their pristine enclosures. But today it's his daughter Daniela, an elegant woman with tousled blond hair, who now runs the *acetaia*, who welcomes us with a warm smile.

We enter the large house, red brick and large windows overlooking a broad and lush valley. Groves of grassparossa and salamino grapes tumble down the hillside in neat rows. Daniela leads me into the kitchen, where her father's hunting dog trophies still fill a shelf over the kitchen counter, tarnished brass cups with heavy marble bases. On the counter sits a good quarter wheel of Parmigiano-Reggiano cheese, a platter of fuzzy just-picked peaches, and a plate of *salame casalingo*, housemade salami. Daniela's mother, Luisa, Sante's widow, is there too, preparing a light *pranzo*, a light lunch; her famous lasagna is cooking in the oven. Like everything else here, the touch of the past can be felt gently pressing on the present. On the mantel of the white stucco fireplace across the room, a World War II German helmet that was found in the vineyards, a feather stuck in the bullet hole, sits next to a framed photograph of Sante

LEFT: Balsamic batteria at Delizia Estense, Montegibbio di Modena, Italy

and a small painting of the Crucifixion. Family photographs hang on the wall. And on the large kitchen table I find what started my friendship with the Bertoni family, small glass bottles of deeply flavorful balsamic vinegar of Modena.

It was no easy task to find the Bertoni family twenty years ago. Then, Alberto combed his resources and tasted a seemingly endless array of productions in search of an honest producer who took the time necessary to nurture the casks of cooked must (unfermented grape juice) to create the true balsamic, unadulterated by caramel or other additives. He found what he was looking for in Bertoni, and we'd been coming here to visit ever since, each of us looking forward to these visits like one expecting to be reunited with a distant relative.

Every visit to the Bertoni family begins with pranzo in the family kitchen, and today is no different. Daniela pours us a glass of homemade lambrusco while her sister Paola has broken off chunks of Parmigiano, the delicate crystals visible to the naked eye. Drawing from a slender-necked glass bottle that contains the *extravecchio*, the super-aged vinegar, she pours a tablespoon of vinegar atop the cheese. It provides a silken flavor to the sharp, almost rudeness of the Parmigiano. The meal has begun.

Though balsamic vinegar was introduced to the United States only in the late 1970s, balsamic vinegar and its precursors have flourished in Italy since ancient times. Roman texts mention *sapa*, a condiment made, like balsamic, from cooked grape must, which is still used in Modenese cooking. Balsamic itself has long been used not just for its culinary wonder but as a health aid. After all, *balsamico* means "balm." Modena has been the center of balsamic vinegar production ever since Francesco I d'Este, the duke of nearby Modena, was cast into exile and built the stunning Ducal Palace in the city center in 1598. With his arrival came the extraordinary wealth of his court—seen in the extravagant palace, now home to the Italian Military Academy—and the associated love

of all things delightful. With Francesco's support, balsamic vinegar began to take a more rarefied form. In fact, Francesco built an acetaia right into the palace tower. Vinegar continued to be refined and codified with the support of generations of dukes until 1796, when upon occupying the city, Napoleon Bonaparte sold off the duke's barrels to local wealthy families. This began the tradition in which families, both wealthy and not, turned their own attics into small *acetaie*. These barrels were passed down for generations to make new vinegar. In fact, during World War II, many families strapped their barrels onto their bicycles as they fled the German advance.

Though now producing on a larger scale, the Bertoni family is a part of the living tradition of balsamic vinegar. For years, Sante, who made his living cleaning ceramic equipment, aged his own balsamic in the family's house in town. But in 1977, he bought this abandoned property with no running water or electricity and its vineyards—twenty acres on steep hills—with the idea of making lambrusco and vinegar. (Plus, as Daniela remembers, he had four daughters and a dozen dogs, and all needed a place to run around.) Sheltered from the heat by the altitude but exposed to the wind, the vineyards are the ideal location for vinegar production, and so he began making balsamic vinegar. Laughing about it now, Daniela recalls, "We called it the *lungo progetto*. The long project, and that it is."

For all its haywire freedom, for all of Italians' elastic notions of time, the Italian government is punctilious when it comes to protecting its culinary traditions. The country is a patchwork of appellations that apply to everything from cheese to wine to olive oil to balsamic vinegar. Traditional balsamic vinegar, for instance, the kind that the Bertoni family makes at Delizia Estense, must follow a raft of minute regulations. In fact, in the family's kitchen, displayed in a frame like a married couple might display the Serenity Prayer, is the definition for the DOCG of balsamic vinegar, written in ornate calligraphy (translated):

RIGHT: Parmigiano and balsamic, il Buco Alimentari FOLLOWING: Roberto, Delizia Estense, Montegibbio di Modena

Natural balsamic vinegar is a product in the area of the ancient exquisite domains and obtained from cooked grape must, matured by slow acidification and derived from natural fermentation and by progressive concentration through a very long series of aging in small wood barrels and addition of aromatic substances.

Dark brown and shiny, the density shall be a smooth syrup.

The scent shall be complex and penetrating, evident but pleasant and harmonious acidity. The taste, traditional and inimitable, shall be well balanced, sweet and sour taste, generously full, savory with velvety nuances in harmony with the olfactory characteristics that are proper to it.

Before lunch, Daniela leads me across the gravel courtyard to a large warehouse that contains the *batterie*, the all-important barrels. There's a small altar in front. She pulls open the doors, and at once we're greeted with the sweet tangy smell of aging vinegar. There's nothing quite like the smell of an acetaia, pungent and so thick you feel you can cut through the perfume.

Inside the cavernous room, rows of barrels are arranged in neat aisles. Each set of batterie consists of ten barrels of diminishing size, each row like a neat set of brass weights or nesting dolls. Each barrel bears the insignia, burned on its head, of F. Renzi, one of Modena's most established barrel makers. Light streams in from the wall of windows overlooking the valley, and as it hits the rows of wooden barrels, they seem to come alive with golden caramel color. Daniela walks through the aisles, holding a glass tube called the wine thief, with which she samples the aging vinegar. Once a year, usually in the autumn or early spring when it's not too hot or cold, Daniela and her family bottle the oldest of the vinegar, transferring the younger liquid down the line of barrels. As Daniela

explains, each barrel is made of a different type of native wood, and each wood gives to the vinegar inside a specific quality. According to the regulations, vinegar makers *must* include oak, chestnut, acacia, cherry, mulberry, ash, and juniper. But they do have some freedom, in terms of which barrels to use and when. There is no set order for how the wood is used or for how long the vinegar must sit in each, just that to be designated Balsamic Vinegar DOC, it must be in a barrel for no fewer than twelve years.

Like many barrel-aged products, balsamic vinegar becomes richer with time. This alchemical process of breathing through wood over time can't be rushed and it can't be faked. It is nearly a living thing, as it travels through the barrels, gleaning from cherry, sweetness; from chestnut, color; and from juniper, strong aromatics. "If we start with one hundred liters of cooked grape must," says Daniela, "we'll end up with only two liters of vinegar."

As Daniela walks past the same barrels Sante did, it occurs to me that these barrels, and their contents, must be a daily reminder of her father. She leads me up a tightly wound spiral staircase into the attic, where she holds the oldest, most precious barrels of balsamico, the extravecchio. Unlike wine, the best of which is kept in temperate cellars, the best balsamic vinegar comes from the attic, a part of the house coldest in the winter and warmest in the summer. These barrels, held in racks under the eaved roof, are from 1987, the first year in which Sante began production and when Daniela was roughly fifteen years old. They've been in barrel for thirty-three years, growing richer and darker with each season. Now, as she walks in her father's footsteps, I can almost feel the weight in each step. Last, a visit to Sante's final creation—a vaulted-ceilinged warehouse-size space filled with the largest barrels of the young balsamic, soaring wooden beams above—seals in the emptiness of the loss and the enormous job that continues tirelessly in its wake. But continue it does, with the diligent help of the entire family.

LEFT: Daniela Bertoni's plum crostata, torta d'albicocche, and digestifs, Delizia Estense FOLLOWING, CLOCKWISE FROM TOP LEFT: Roberto Paris; Barrel #81; vineyards at Delizia Estense; Paola and Daniela Bertoni; sauvignon blanc grapes; Daniela Bertoni checking the batterie; balsamic barrel; Daniela Bertoni and son; grapevines, Delizie Estense; batteria, Delizia Estense; Donna pulls balsamic sample; barrel detail

We head back to the family kitchen for coffee, beautiful crostatas, and fresh peaches. Paola brings in a box of the balsamic tradizionale and uncorks the precious bottle. The silky liquid is lustrous, the color of mahogany. The balsamic has a depth hard to describe. It comes in gentle waves of sweetness and acidity, not too much of either. It provides the silken texture and bittersweet flavor of the perfect digestif, reminding us that centuries ago this was the ultimate end to a meal and still is today.

The taste lingers on the tongue, changing as the afternoon light casts upon the kitchen wall. To taste true balsamic vinegar, compared with caramel-colored artificial imitations, is like swimming in an ocean rather than splashing in a puddle. The flavors are deep, with a balanced acidity, the beauty immediate, the richness vast.

On Bond Street, we use balsamic vinegar much as Daniela and thousands of Modenese do. We drizzle it over irregular chunks of Parmigiano-Reggiano cheese to start a meal or over lightly macerated strawberries to end it. We use it as a glaze for poultry or game such as quail or on a beautiful grilled radicchio salad. There's no better dessert that I know of than fresh panna cotta drizzled with balsamic, Alberto's favorite classic (page 274). With a flavor so deeply textured, balsamic can dance with many partners. Along with olive oil and salt, vinegar completes the sacred trilogy of the Mediterranean. So for our dearest customers, there's often a demi-tasse full of our own vinegar from the batterie at the end of the meal, the ideal digestif.

Sixteen years ago, when we first opened il Buco Alimentari, Sante presented me with a series of seven batterie from Delizia Estense, a full complement of oak, chestnut, acacia, cherry, mulberry, ash, and juniper in decreasing size. We filled them with Sante's ten- and twenty-year-old vinegar and installed them right in the center of the dining room. And, just like Sante did before and Daniela does now, every autumn, when it's chilly but not cold, we rotate the vinegar from one barrel to the next, adding character, depth, and flavor with time.

I hold close the batterie at il Buco, Sante and Daniela Bertoni, and the entire story of balsamic vinegar. Not just for the beautiful vinegar they produce or even the warm sense of the rough-hewn world you can get only from a barrel, but because they embody a story of families working together through generations, motivated not by commerce but by passion and quality, to produce from humble ingredients a product of immense richness. Every day when I walk into Alimentari, I see the barrels and think of my friend Sante and his family now and how the vinegar inside will always connect us. It's a bittersweet and beautiful thought.

RIGHT: Donna and Daniela in vineyards

PRIMI PIATTI

———

EGG PASTA DOUGH

This simple pasta dough can be used for any egg-based pasta, including ravioli, pappardelle, and spaghetti. The combination of the 00 flour and eggs yields a beautifully silken texture, whether you use a traditional crank pasta machine or the pasta-making attachment to your stand mixer. All of the pasta at il Buco and Alimentari is made with the deft and steady hand of Bertha Gonzalez.

Serves 4 to 6

200 grams 00 flour
120 grams durum flour
30 grams semolina flour
3 grams fine sea salt
2 large eggs
3 large egg yolks
1 tablespoon extra virgin olive oil

1. In a large bowl, sift together the flours and salt.

2. In a small bowl, whisk together the eggs, yolks, and olive oil. Then combine the egg mixture with the flour mixture in the large bowl, either with your hands (if you don't mind a little mess) or with a wooden spoon until incorporated. If the dough looks dry, add a dash more of olive oil. If it looks wet, a dash of flour. (Alternatively, form a mound of the sifted-together flours and salt directly on your work surface. Using your hands, form a crater in the middle, add egg yolks, eggs, and olive oil. Using your fingers, gradually incorporate the flour into this mixture, kneading until a dough is formed.)

3. If using a bowl, turn the dough onto a well-floured work surface (if not, just continue on the board) and knead for 4 to 5 minutes, until the dough is smooth. Wrap the dough in plastic wrap and let rest it at room temperature for an hour (or in a fridge overnight.)

4. When ready to use, divide the dough into four equal balls. Rewrap the dough not being used so it doesn't dry out.

5. Starting on the widest setting, crank the pasta dough through the pasta maker. Laying the dough on a well-floured work surface, fold the dough in half, and pass through the machine again. Do this two or three times until the dough is smooth.

6. Now start decreasing the width of the rollers, cranking the dough through each level at least once. Stop when the appropriate thickness, about $\frac{1}{16}$-inch thick for noodles, or $\frac{1}{32}$-inch thick for a filled pasta, is reached. Alternatively, using a rolling pin on a well-floured surface, roll the dough out to a similar thickness. (You should be able to read a newspaper through the dough when it is being used for filled pasta.)

7. Store the finished pasta dough in a single layer on a parchment paper–lined baking sheet, covered with a kitchen towel to keep moist.

RAVIOLI DI RICOTTA

When Jody Williams arrived in 1998, il Buco took a hard turn toward Italy from Spain. Jody had staged at Caffè Arti e Mestieri in Reggio Emilia, where she had perfected recipes like this: simple, divine, and delicious. She had such a beautiful hand with pasta, as is clear to anyone who has eaten at Via Carota or I Sodi, the restaurants she now runs with her partner, Rita Sodi. Back when she was with us, I lived on and for these little ricotta pillows, adorned simply with the trinity of Italian cuisine: tomato, basil, and olive oil.

Serves 4

1 quart store-bought or fresh ricotta (page 58)
3 large eggs
⅛ teaspoon grated nutmeg
Zest of 1 lemon
1½ teaspoons fine sea salt, divided
1 recipe fresh pasta dough (page 180), not rolled out
3 tablespoons extra virgin olive oil, plus more
    for serving
2 garlic cloves, sliced
1 pint cherry tomatoes
Freshly ground black pepper
½ bunch basil, chopped, with a few sprigs reserved
Parmigiano-Reggiano, for finishing

1. Make the filling for the ravioli by whisking together the ricotta, 2 eggs, nutmeg, lemon zest, and 1 teaspoon salt in a large bowl until uniform. Place the filling in a pastry bag with a plain tip or a ziptop bag with a corner cut off. Set aside in the refrigerator.

2. To make the ravioli, roll out the dough per the instructions on page 180, making two identical-size sheets roughly 6 inches wide. The dough should be thin enough that it is nearly translucent, but strong enough to hold filling.

3. Break the remaining egg into a ramekin and scramble with a fork. Using a pastry brush, lightly brush one side of one of the sheets of pasta dough.

4. Using the piping bag, pipe half dollar–size dollops of the filling onto the egg-washed pasta dough into 2 rows about 4 inches apart. Carefully drape the second sheet of pasta dough on top.

5. Seal the dough together first around the mounds of filling by using your fingers to gently push out any excess air. Then, using a pasta wheel or a sharp knife, cut the pasta evenly between the mounds of ricotta to make squares. Press around the edges of each ravioli with fingers to ensure a good seal.

6. To make the tomato sauce, heat a large heavy-bottomed skillet over medium heat. Add the olive oil and heat to a shimmer. Add the garlic and cook until golden, 1 to 2 minutes. Add the tomatoes and cook until they burst, 5 to 10 minutes. Season with ½ teaspoon of salt and pepper to taste, and stir in the chopped basil. Remove from the heat.

7. Meanwhile bring a large pot of salted water to boil. Add the ravioli and cook for approximately 4 minutes or until they float. Remove each ravioli with a spider or slotted spoon directly into the skillet with the tomato sauce. Reserve ½ cup of pasta water.

8. Reheat the ravioli and tomato sauce over gentle heat, adding a bit of pasta water only if the sauce seems too dry.

9. To serve, divide into four bowls, top with freshly shaved Parmigiano-Reggiano, a drizzle of olive oil, and the basil sprigs.

BUCATINI CACIO E PEPE

One of the perennial bestsellers at il Buco Alimentari is also one of the simplest: bucatini cacio e pepe. *Cacio* is a local Roman dialect for "cheese"; here, a pecorino romano, a soft sheep's milk cheese made in the area since ancient times. *Pepe* is "pepper." And that's about it, really. There's no fussy technique here, just the naturally occurring magic between fat and hot water.

This recipe takes me back more than twenty years when I went to Rome to visit a film producer friend of mine, Alberto Leotti. Alberto picked me up on his Vespa and whisked me over the cobblestones into the historic center of the city to a tiny restaurant in Lampante called Cacio e Pepe. The red-and-white-cloth-clad tables on the street outside were filled with locals enjoying classic Roman cuisine: fried artichokes (page 33), little potato dumplings called *chicce*, veal *alla fornara*, and, of course, bowls piled high with creamy pasta flecked with pepper: cacio e pepe. We waited and waited and eventually Alberto and I got a seat and ordered a couple of glasses of Morellino

Scansano and two bowls of pasta. The namesake cacio e pepe was unforgettably good: the pasta was perfectly al dente, the pepper gave the dish some muscle, and the pecorino contributed an indulgent creaminess.

Years later, when Justin Smillie made cacio e pepe for me the first time at Alimentari, I was right back in that café in Rome. At Alimentari, we use a pasta shape called bucatini, which is like spaghetti's thicker, heartier cousin, but with a hollow center (*bucatini* means "little holes"). Not only is the pasta coated in sauce, but the sauce gets inside the tube too. We get our bucatini from Setaro, a third generation *pastificio* in Torre Annunziata, a small town in Naples where the warm sea breeze allows the pasta to dry naturally and gently.

Natural and gentle is also a good way to describe the secret to making cacio e pepe, since almost the entire preparation is done off the flame, gliding by on the residual heat of the pasta water. It's a brilliant, economical, and delicious dish, an Alimentari favorite since day one.

Serves 4

Sea salt to taste
1 pound dried bucatini
1¼ cups (4 ounces) freshly grated
    Parmigiano-Reggiano
1 cup (3 ounces) shaved pecorino romano,
    plus additional for finishing
6 tablespoons unsalted butter, cubed and at
    room temperature
3 tablespoons coarsely ground black pepper,
    plus additional for finishing
4 teaspoons olive oil

1. Bring a large pot of salted water to a boil. Once boiling, add the bucatini.

2. While the pasta is cooking, add the Parmigiano, pecorino, room temperature butter, pepper, and olive

oil to a large bowl and mix to create a paste. Smooth the paste around the bottom of the bowl and reserve near the cooking pasta.

3. When the pasta is al dente (after approximately 9 minutes), use a pair of tongs to remove the pasta directly from the pasta pot into the bowl with the cheese mixture. (Do not drain noodles in a colander; the clinging pasta water is vital to the dish.) Stir vigorously until the noodles are well coated in the pungent cheese mixture. If the sauce is too tight and sticky, add more pasta water from the pot, a little bit at a time (a little goes a long way). It should be luscious and creamy.

4. Divide into 4 bowls, and finish with additional pecorino and pepper.

PAPPARDELLE CON PORCINI

When porcini come into season in Italy, I run to La Cantina—the restaurant Alberto built in Spello—where these gorgeous fungi are grilled over fire and drizzled with Moraiolo olive oil. The next course is pappardelle con porcini. What I love so much about this dish, even more than the earthy flavor of the porcini layered between delicate strips of fresh pasta, is that it demonstrates how little we have to do to what is naturally delicious. Porcini mushrooms grow all over Europe, Asia, and North America. As autumn travels around the world, mushroom lovers and gourmets head to the forests to forage. Porcini are both common and unusually suited for cooking. It's so satisfying to find a cluster, with their thick stems and jaunty caps, but even more satisfying is getting them back to the kitchen. Here, we do relatively little to the porcini other than showcase their natural flavor with a bit of thyme, garlic, and the similarly nutty *pecorino di noce*, which has spent months wrapped in walnut leaves.

Serves 4

1 recipe fresh pasta dough (page 180)

Sea salt to taste

3 tablespoons extra virgin olive oil

¾ pound fresh porcini mushrooms, cleaned, trimmed, and sliced ⅛ inch thick

1 garlic clove, thinly sliced

2 sprigs thyme or nepitella, leaves chopped

1 tablespoon unsalted butter

4 tablespoons pecorino di noce or Parmigiano-Reggiano, finely grated

1 teaspoon freshly cracked black pepper

Torn fresh parsley, for garnish

1. Following instructions on page 180, roll out the pasta dough and cut it into strips approximately ¾-inch wide.

2. Heat the olive oil in a large skillet over medium heat until shimmering. Add the mushrooms to the skillet and allow them to brown, undisturbed, for about 2 minutes. Once the mushrooms begin to brown, add in the garlic and cook for an additional 2 minutes, allowing it to turn golden. Stir in the thyme or nepitella.

3. Meanwhile bring a large pot of salted water to a boil. Add the fresh pappardelle and cook until just al dente, approximately 3 minutes. Drain the pasta but retain ¼ cup of the pasta cooking water.

4. Add the reserved pasta water to the skillet with mushrooms and stir. Then add the cooked pasta to the skillet and toss over low heat. Add butter for shine, and about half the cheese. Toss to coat again.

5. To plate, divide the pasta among four bowls. Top with cracked black pepper, parsley, and the rest of the cheese.

"I can always count on beautifully fresh ingredients and dreamy meals, as if I've walked into a perpetual Italian country feast."

—SCOTT COHEN

PASTA CON LE VONGOLE

Even before I was connected with il Buco, my fiancé, Joe Rosato, and I used to make pasta con le vongole in our tiny New York apartment, using canned clams with clam juice and white wine. I loved it. Cooking with Joe was always a joy. The first time I had *real* pasta con le vongole using fresh clams was by the seaside in the Marche with Alberto. After a long day in the sun, starving, we strolled into a no-nonsense trattoria by the water. It was a revelation: the salinity of the tiny clams, called *vongole veraci*, the sturdy kick of the garlic, the emulsified olive oil holding the firm pasta to the clams. It's been a staple whenever I entertain at my house out East and is one of my dad's all-time favorites. Because the real vongole veraci don't exist on this side of the Atlantic, I often substitute New Zealand cockles for clams; they're just the right size, intensely briny with beautiful striated shells.

Serves 4

Sea salt to taste
2 tablespoons olive oil, plus additional for finishing
2 garlic cloves, smashed
Peperoncino to taste
1 small bunch parsley, chopped
4 pounds cockles, cleaned and purged*
1 pound dried spaghetti
Lemon juice to taste

To purge the cockles, soak them in salted water in the fridge for a few hours to draw out the sand.

1. Bring a large pot of salted water to boil.

2. In a large skillet, heat 2 tablespoons of olive oil over medium heat until shimmering. Add the garlic and sauté until golden but not burned. Add the crushed peperoncino to taste, half of the parsley, and the cockles. Cover the skillet and cook, shaking the pan every once in a while, until the cockles pop open, 10 to 15 minutes. Discard the garlic cloves after cooking.

3. Meanwhile, add the spaghetti to the boiling water and cook until al dente. Drain the pasta (reserving a small amount of the pasta water) and add to the skillet with the now-open cockles. Toss to coat. Only add the reserved pasta water if the cockles do not provide enough juice to the pan to coat the noodles. You may want to remove a number of the cockles from the shells to make eating more enjoyable. (Careful, they're hot.) Finish with the remaining parsley, a drizzle of olive oil, and a squeeze of lemon juice.

PASTA CON LE SARDE

I don't think there's any pasta preparation that captures Palermo as much as this lovely combination of sea and land flavors. As the name suggests, pasta con le sarde features the wonderfully fresh sardines one sees in such astonishing array at Ballaro, the expansive fish market. But what endears the dish to me is the fennel pollen, whose fragrant aroma balances the strong oiliness of the fish, as well as the addition of pine nuts and raisins. According to culinary legend, these typically North African ingredients found their way into the Sicilian canon and into this preparation in particular after the Arab chef of Euphemius, a ninth-century Byzantine commander, made it for his hungry troops stationed in Sicily. The toasted breadcrumbs are a later addition but a wonderful one too.

....

Serves 4

2 tablespoons pine nuts
¼ cup breadcrumbs
2 tablespoons golden raisins
Sea salt to taste
1 pound dried busiate or bucatini
¼ cup plus 3 tablespoons extra virgin
    olive oil, divided
1 white onion, thinly sliced
1 fennel bulb, grated or thinly sliced on a
    mandoline, fronds reserved for garnish
5 anchovy fillets, packed in olive oil
2 garlic cloves, finely minced
2 tablespoons salted capers, soaked and drained
Peperoncino to taste
¼ cup white wine
8 fresh sardines (about 14 ounces), cleaned
    and deboned
1 teaspoon finely chopped parsley
1 teaspoon fennel pollen
Freshly ground black pepper to taste

1. Preheat the oven to 275°F. Spread the pine nuts evenly on one sheet pan, the breadcrumbs on another. Toast both for 5 minutes and remove just before they start to color.

2. Soak the raisins in a bowl of warm water until plump, approximately 8 minutes. Drain.

3. Bring a large pot of salted water to boil. Once boiling, add the bucatini. Cook until al dente, approximately 10 minutes, occasionally stirring.

4. Meanwhile, in a saucepan over medium-low heat, heat ¼ cup of the olive oil until shimmering. Add the onion and cook until translucent. Then add the fennel, anchovies, garlic, capers, and peperoncino and cook for 5 to 7 minutes, stirring occasionally.

5. Add the raisins, white wine, and ¼ cup of the pasta water; continue tossing. Once well mixed, add the sardines, parsley, fennel pollen, and pine nuts and allow to cook for an additional 2 minutes. Drizzle with an additional 3 tablespoons olive oil. The sardines will break into small pieces and incorporate into the sauce. Remove from the heat and allow the flavors to commingle for a few minutes.

6. Drain the pasta and add to the saucepan with the sauce; toss to combine. Season with salt and pepper if needed.

7. To serve, divide the pasta equally among four bowls. Sprinkle with breadcrumbs and fennel fronds to finish.

SPAGHETTI ALLA BOTTARGA

I'll never forget my trip on the back of Alberto's bright yellow BMW R1100S along the coast of Sardegna from the northeast down to see my "family" in Cagliari. We turned the point and headed up the west coast from Cagliari to Oristano, the cradle of bottarga production. The farm where the grey mullet ovarian sacs in various gradations of amber lay air-curing in uneven rows was a spectacle to behold. Alberto revered this delicacy of the sea and shaved it into thin slivers over celery with a remarkable fresh Sardinian olive oil (page 100): the epitome of three ingredients on a plate in perfect harmony.

But grey mullet bottarga also pairs perfectly with pasta. On the island of Salina, one of the Aeolian Islands, a simple spit of land off the coast of Sicily, I had another deceptively simple rendition of this unique ingredient. I was invited to a tiny restaurant where the bottarga was simply shaved over bucatini with just a hint of garlic, olive oil, and lemon zest. It was sublime: the perfect blend of salt and sea in the middle of the Mediterranean. It has been a staple at Alimentari since the early days, where we have also paired it with squid ink spaghetti to add another level of complexity and texture. Please don't confuse it with *bottarga di tonno* (tuna bottarga), also used extensively in Sicily but with a much more pungent, salty result.

Serves 4

Sea salt to taste
1 pound dried spaghetti
¼ cup extra virgin olive oil
2 garlic cloves, minced
2 tablespoons chopped parsley
1 peperoncino, crushed, or to taste
8 ounces bottarga di muggine, grated
Zest and juice of 1 small lemon

1. Bring a large pot of well-salted water to boil. Add the pasta and cook until al dente (7 to 8 minutes).

2. While the pasta is cooking, heat the olive oil in a cast iron skillet over medium heat. Once shimmering, add the garlic and cook until translucent, 3 to 4 minutes. Add the parsley and crushed peperoncino to taste. Ladle out ¼ cup of the pasta water and add to the pan and incorporate. Remove the skillet from the heat.

3. Drain the pasta, reserving a bit more pasta water. Add the pasta to the skillet, tossing to coat, being careful not to break the noodles.

4. Fold in the bottarga. Sauce should emulsify the bottarga with the pasta. It should be creamy; if dry, add a bit more pasta water and fold into the noodles.

5. Divide into four bowls, season with the fresh lemon juice, lemon zest, a few extra gratings of bottarga, and a pinch of salt to taste, and serve immediately.

"In planning our restaurant in Marfa, Texas, we sat down at table 6 for what we call a long, boozy lunch. Instead of dwindling into dinner, we woke up in Iceland looking for the northern lights."

—ROCKY BARNETT &
VIRGINIA LEBERMAN

PAN ROASTED GNOCCHI

Angelo Scolastra, Alberto's mentor, was perhaps one of the best cooks I have ever met. After his wife Sandra passed away, Angelo's daughter Luisa took the reins of the kitchen at Villa Roncalli. Today, she runs the kitchen with a tiny team of three ladies, preparing multicourse feasts eaten by candlelight. If you step into the kitchen, Luisa is a blur of activity under the steady gaze of her father, who looks down from a portrait above the door. I've never seen a measuring cup or a tablespoon. She cooks by feel, using her senses, and her heart. On a recent trip back, I saw her make gnocchi à la minute. I was blown away at how speedily she turned a pot of skinned boiled potatoes into a snake of gnocchi, then into bite-size pillows.

One of the cardinal rules of the Scolastra family is to use what you have. This recipe relies on the mushrooms foraged near Foligno, but you can use any that you find in a farmers' market. The caramelization of the mushrooms and the crust of the pan roasted gnocchi are textural nuances brought to Alimentari by Chef Justin Smillie, bringing an entirely new sensation to this classic dish.

Serves 4

2 pounds large russet potatoes
1½ cups coarse sea salt
2 cups 00 flour, plus additional for rolling
1 teaspoon fine sea salt, plus additional to taste
1 large egg, lightly beaten
2 tablespoons olive oil, divided
4 tablespoons unsalted butter, divided, plus
    additional for finishing
8 ounces mixed wild mushrooms, cleaned, trimmed,
    and torn into large pieces
8 sage leaves, roughly torn
2 small shallots, finely diced
4 ounces grated Parmigiano-Reggiano, plus
    additional shavings for garnish
Freshly ground black pepper to taste

1. Preheat the oven to 400°F. Place the potatoes on a sheet pan covered in coarse sea salt. Roast for 45 minutes until fork tender. Allow to cool.

2. Peel the potatoes and pass through the finest setting of a ricer into a large bowl.

3. Spread the potatoes out on a lightly floured work surface. In a small bowl, mix the flour and the fine sea salt. Pour over the top of the potatoes. Drizzle the egg on top. Slowly cut into the dough with a bench scraper and continue until fully incorporated. Knead the mass gently until the outside is slightly crumbly, still aerated. Divide the dough into 8 pieces. Roll each piece into a 24-inch-long rope about ½ inch thick. Cut into ¾- to 1-inch pieces, dust with flour, and arrange in a single layer on a lightly floured rimmed baking sheet. Transfer to the freezer for at least 3 hours, or overnight for best results.

4. Remove the gnocchi from the freezer, then prepare them in two batches (or two pans simultaneously). For each batch (or pan), heat 1 tablespoon each olive oil and butter over medium until shimmering. Once the butter begins to foam, add half of the gnocchi and cook untouched for 2 to 3 minutes. The tops will begin to rise like a soufflé and a golden brown crust will start to form. Add half of the mushrooms, sage, and shallots and toss gently for 2 minutes. Pour off the excess fat. Add a splash of water, 1 tablespoon butter, and half the Parmigiano, remove from heat, and toss until glazed.

5. Portion gently into four bowls, then top with the pepper to taste, and a few shavings of Parmigiano.

SQUID INK RISOTTO

When squid ink is used to make a pasta, it is often incorporated into the dough itself. But in this preparation from the Veneto, the ink is tossed with the arborio rice, and the result is a striking midnight-black risotto. Studded with rings of squid and their tentacles—as if straight from a Venetian lagoon—the risotto is a bit crunchier than the creamy version you might be used to, balanced by the sweet acidity of the tomato, invisible in the black ink but nevertheless present.

....

Serves 4

6 medium squid, fresh or frozen, cleaned
    (approximately ¾ pound)
2 lemons
3 tablespoons extra virgin olive oil,
    divided, plus more for drizzling
½ bulb fennel, minced (about 1 cup)
1 medium white onion, diced
2 garlic cloves, finely diced
1 teaspoon tomato paste
½ teaspoon fine sea salt, plus
    additional for finishing
1 cup dry white wine
1½ cups carnaroli or arborio rice
4 tablespoons squid ink
1 teaspoon unsalted butter
½ teaspoon Espelette pepper

1. To prepare the squid, cut off the tentacles and halve if very large. Cut the squid bodies into ¼-inch-thick rings. Set aside.

2. Peel and juice the lemons, reserving peels.

3. In a large high-sided saucepan heat 2 tablespoons olive oil over medium-high heat until shimmering. Add the fennel, onion, garlic, tomato paste, and salt, stirring gently. After 5 minutes, add the white wine, then let reduce over low heat for an additional 5 minutes, until almost evaporated.

4. Add rice to the pan and incorporate. Then add 1 cup of water to the rice, and stir until absorbed. Continue to add ½ cup of water at a time as the rice absorbs the liquid, stirring all the time. The whole process will take approximately 20 minutes and you will need to add up to another 3 to 4 cups of water. The rice should remain al dente.

5. Add the lemon peel, squid ink, butter, and Espelette and incorporate. Then add the squid and the remaining tablespoon of olive oil and let cook for a final 5 minutes. Remove and discard the lemon peel. Finish with the lemon juice to taste.

6. To serve, divide among the serving dishes and finish with sea salt.

"At first Donna opened an antiques store and would occasionally invite someone to lunch. Once I asked if they could do a meal for ten. They shoved a few of the worn, wooden tables together. Everyone loved the food. So they constructed a proper kitchen and opened a restaurant!"

—CHUCK CLOSE

NETTLE RISOTTO

Cooking with nettles has always intrigued me. There's something a little transgressive about eating a plant that, if you even brush up against it in the wild, leaves you with a painful rash. But one reason, perhaps, the nettle evolved to be so unfriendly is that it is in fact so delicious to eat. Like so much of Italy's cuisine, cooking with *ortiche*, or stinging nettles, arose at the intersection of necessity and availability. (Stinging nettles also grow wild all across North America.) But today we go out of our way to source them. With a flavor resting between a vegetable and an herb and a sublime color, they're like a gutsier, brighter spinach. Here they are the perfect foil for the sweetness of goat cheese.

Serves 4

4 bunches fresh nettles (approximately ½ pound)
3 tablespoons extra virgin olive oil
2 tablespoons unsalted butter
1 medium white onion, diced
2 cups carnaroli or arborio rice
½ cup dry white wine
3 ounces fresh goat cheese
½ teaspoon fine sea salt, plus additional for finishing
2 tablespoons grated Parmigiano-Reggiano

1. While wearing a pair of protective gloves, prepare the nettles by separating the leaves from the stalks. Discard the stalks and set the leaves aside.

2. Bring 2 cups of water to a rolling boil. Prepare an ice bath by filling a medium-size bowl with ice and cold water.

3. Blanch the nettle leaves in the water for 30 seconds to 1 minute until bright green, then, using tongs, plunge the leaves into the ice bath. Reserve ½ cup of the nettle cooking water. Once cool, wring out the leaves to remove any excess liquid. Chop finely and set aside. No need for gloves once the nettles are cooked.

4. For the risotto, add the olive oil and butter to a large saucepan over medium heat. When the butter begins to foam, add the onions, stirring as they soften, not allowing them to color, approximately 5 minutes. Gently add the rice, stirring together with the onions, allowing the fat to bind the two together.

5. Add the wine in a steady stream and cook for 2 to 3 minutes, stirring constantly. Then add the reserved nettle cooking water, stirring constantly until absorbed. Add ½ cup plain water and repeat the process. Continue to add ½ cup of water at a time as the rice dries out and plumps up during cooking, stirring all the time. The whole process will take approximately 25 minutes and you will need to add another 3 to 4 cups of water. The rice should remain al dente.

6. Finally, add the goat cheese and the salt and stir until incorporated. Fold in the nettles. Just before serving, fold in the Parmigiano-Reggiano, to help bind the risotto together.

7. To serve, divide the risotto equally among four plates and serve immediately. Finish with sea salt.

TORCHIO WITH BROCCOLINI

Torchio is a sophisticated twist on fusilli. It's an extruded pasta, which means it's pushed through a press. The name is a bit of a mystery: the spiral shape itself resembles an early mechanical piece of machinery used for pressing grapes for wine, or for printing presses. Regardless of what it's named after, the cup-shaped curved pieces are wonderful holders for sauce. And what better combination than broccolini with some meaty bacon made from a pig cheek?

Serves 4

Sea salt to taste
1 pound torchio (or fusilli, penne, or rigatoni)
2 tablespoons olive oil
6 ounces guanciale, julienned
1 bunch (12 ounces) broccolini, trimmed and
    roughly chopped
2 garlic cloves, chopped
Peperoncino to taste
¼ cup (4 ounces) finely shaved pecorino toscano,
    plus additional for finishing

1. Bring a medium-size pot of salted water to a boil. Add the pasta, cooking for 8 to 9 minutes or until al dente.

2. Meanwhile, heat 1 tablespoon olive oil in a large skillet over medium-high heat. Once shimmering, add the guanciale and cook, stirring constantly until crisp, approximately 2 minutes.

3. Carefully drain all but ½ tablespoon fat from the pan, then the add the broccolini, garlic, and peperoncino, letting it brown, approximately 2 minutes. Drain the pasta, reserving ½ cup pasta water.

4. Add ¼ cup reserved pasta water to the pan. Allow it to cook down for 2 to 3 minutes, stirring gently. Add a bit more pasta water only if sauce seems too dry.

5. Once the liquid is reduced, add the cooked pasta, the remaining tablespoon of olive oil, and pecorino and toss, still over heat, for 3 to 4 minutes.

6. To serve, equally divide the pasta among four bowls. Top with additional pecorino.

"I've been going to il Buco as long as it's been open… You can find me on the corner of the bar at 3:30 most afternoons having a late lunch, eating delicious food, feeling satisfied and loved."

—JOHN DERIAN

PACCHERI WITH LAMB SUGO

Paccheri, akin to jumbo rigatoni, has its origins in Campania, and the name comes from *una pacca*, which means "a slap" in the local dialect. Allegedly, these large tubes were used by Italian garlic farmers to smuggle their superior garlic into the Prussian market in the early 1600s. Up to four large cloves could fit inside! Today, paccheri is often served with a hearty meat sauce like this lamb sugo that finds its way inside the pasta as well as coating the outside. On a chilly night, it's the most soothing and comforting plate you can imagine.

Serves 4 to 6

2 cups coarse sea salt, plus additional to taste
1 white onion, quartered, plus another half
4 stalks celery, roughly chopped, divided
Peel of 1 lime
1 head of garlic, cut in half through its middle
2 bay leaves
1 teaspoon black peppercorns
1 teaspoon coriander seeds
½ teaspoon dried juniper berries
½ teaspoon allspice
2 cloves
1 lamb shoulder, approximately 1 pound, deboned
5 tablespoons olive oil, divided
1 carrot, roughly chopped
1 tablespoon tomato paste
1 cup white wine
1 cup canned whole plum tomatoes
24 ounces paccheri
1 teaspoon unsalted butter
⅓ cup grated Parmigiano-Reggiano

1. Make the brine: Place coarse salt, ½ onion, half of the chopped celery, the lime peel, ½ head garlic, and all the spices into 4 quarts of water in a large stockpot and bring to a boil. Remove from the heat and let cool. Rinse the lamb shoulder and let it sit in the brine for 12 hours, refrigerated, to tenderize the meat.

2. Remove the shoulder from the brine and pat dry. Preheat the oven to 350°F.

3. Heat 3 tablespoons of the olive oil until shimmering in a cast iron skillet. Sear the lamb for 6 minutes, then flip and cook for another 6 minutes. Remove and set aside.

4. Heat the remaining 2 tablespoons of olive oil in a dutch oven over medium heat until shimmering. Add the quartered onion, carrot, remaining chopped celery, and the remaining garlic and cook for 5 minutes. Stir in the tomato paste and allow to cook for 2 to 3 minutes. Add the wine and reduce for 5 minutes, then add the canned tomatoes. Reduce for another 5 minutes, stirring occasionally. Add 3 cups of water to the dutch oven and bring to a boil. Once boiling, add the lamb. Cover with foil and place in the oven for 1 hour 45 minutes to 2 hours, until the lamb is fork tender.

5. Remove the pot from the oven and carefully remove the lamb. Strain the liquid into a large pot through a fine-mesh strainer, discarding the solids. Pull the lamb into little pieces and add to the strained liquid.

6. Bring a large pot of salted water to boil. Add the paccheri and cook to al dente, 8 to 9 minutes.

7. Meanwhile, warm the sugo over medium heat in a dutch oven. When the paccheri is done, drain and toss into the sugo and add the butter.

8. Divide the pasta into bowls. Top with the grated Parmigiano-Reggiano and a sprinkle of sea salt to taste, and serve immediately.

XII

SALUMI

——

At its heart, an alimentari *is a place you go to be nourished. All across Italy, in cities, towns, and villages, you'll find these usually mom-and-pop-owned places that do business selling grocery items and simple sandwiches, everything from apples to Kinder eggs to crusty loaves of ciabatta. And it's not an uncommon—but always a very welcome—sight to see, hanging above the delicatessen counters and displayed within them, an array of dried and cured meats—what we call* salumi—*in various shapes and sizes.*

To a newcomer, the sheer variety can be daunting. Some salumi look like classic sausages, link upon link upon link. Some, oddly shaped and wrapped in cheesecloth, are totally unidentifiable. And some, like the venerated prosciutto di Parma, made of the entire hind leg of a pig, are perhaps a little *too* identifiable. There they hang, festooned like prayer flags in the store, announcing that this is a place that will satisfy your hunger. Not every alimentari in Italy—and actually fewer and fewer—makes their own salumi

in-house. It's a costly and time-consuming process. But when we opened il Buco Alimentari e Vineria in 2011, salumi was at the center of the project. In fact, it was the very reason we opened at all.

The planning for Alimentari began in earnest on one of the darkest days of Bernardo Flores's life back in 2006. Today, Bernardo is our salumi master or *salumiere*. Good natured, shy, watchful, a man who keeps his passions cloaked under his hooded eyelids, Bernardo has been with me from nearly the beginning.

LEFT: House cured guanciale, il Buco Alimentari

He arrived in our kitchen twenty years ago, shortly after coming to New York from Puebla, Mexico. He started as a dishwasher, but he was a hard worker and a dependable presence, and soon he worked his way up our loose kitchen hierarchy from dishwasher to salad man to cook.

At the time, Alberto—who can and does go on for hours about the magic of cured meat—was already trying to build our salumi program from the ground up. Like many Italians, especially those from poor rural areas, salumi wasn't a luxury for Alberto or his family growing up. It was a necessity, a way to keep a hog feeding a family for months or even years. Think of Roberto, whose room in the basement of his childhood home stood in as a curing room for the family salumi. If you ask him why he no longer eats pork, he'll tell you of the time he discovered that the salumi hanging from the rafters had been made from his beloved pet pig. Similarly, our first attempt at salumi was a distinctly DIY effort. Alberto invited his friends Salvatore and Efisio, butchers from his hometown of Foligno, to get us started. During lulls in service, Bernardo went downstairs to watch.

He noted how the men broke down half hogs, delivered to us from our friend Mike Yezzi at Flying Pigs Farm in Battenkill Valley. He saw how they separated the animal into its primal cuts and how, unlike American butchers, Salvatore and Efisio cut along the animal's natural seams, preserving the long muscles of the back, belly, leg, and shoulder for curing. And how they extracted from these almost sculptural forms, pink girded in white fat, the meat that would become, in months' time, lonzas, coppas, culatellos, pancettas, prosciuttos, and more. He watched as they coated the meat in salt and let it sit, allowing the crystals to draw out the moisture from the meat itself over time, until it was ready to be hung and, largely, left for up to a year.

One day Alberto, noting how rapt Bernardo was, said, "Bernardo, you aren't going back to the kitchen. You're going to stay here with us and learn." And so

began his education. Gradually, Bernardo learned how to wield the long skinny knives for separating fat from meat. He learned to cut at the joints. He learned that the long loin running along the pig's back is the lonza and the belly is the pancetta and the cheek becomes guanciale and the leg becomes prosciutto or, perhaps, the most rarefied of all salumi, the culatello. Most important, he learned about the alchemical power of salt and time. Back then, we were making mostly prosciutto. It is a large cut and it takes the most time to cure, which means, if done right, the flavors become complex, the meat almost crystallized with nutty overtones, while the fat remains buttery, beautiful silky white.

By the time Salvatore and Efisio returned to Italy a few months later, Bernardo had fully embraced his calling as a salumiere. In a nook of the wine cellar enclosed by glass hung the fruits of his, Salvatore's, and Efisio's work: neat lines of hanging inchoate prosciutto. For a time after they left, Bernardo was happy to continue the tradition as he learned it from them. But he's also a wonderfully curious spirit, and soon he began to experiment too. The process of salumi is at once incredibly simple and very complex. Like any fermentation process from beer to bread, curing meat relies on the natural environment. It is the job of the salumiere to create the correct conditions for the microorganisms to do their work. Salt, time, and meat is all you need, but how much of each you use and how skillfully you use it determines whether the end product will be delicious or, potentially, deadly—a host of deleterious bacteria, from listeria to botulism to salmonella, as well as harmful molds can grow in the whole cuts as well as the ground meat preparations. So Bernardo strictly hewed to temperature and storage controls, as well as adding the minimal amount of sodium nitrates and nitrites to prevent the growth of certain microbes like botulism.

Over the course of a few years, Bernardo perfected his craft, learning to carefully weigh the meat and salt accordingly. He experimented with how much fennel

206

to add in the finocchiona, what type of chili to add to our spicy salami toscano, and how much salt to use for his prosciutto. Because salumi relies on time, these changes were borne out only months later. Alberto and I, as well as the rest of our diners, were impressed with the results. Our salumi board was one of the best sellers at il Buco. We were, as they say, riding high on the hog.

We would continue to develop our program over time. In 2003, my dear friend, food writer Peter Kaminsky—who had written his first Underground Gourmet piece on il Buco in 1994—invited me to tag along on a trip to a Land Stewardship and Sustainability Conference in South Carolina. Peter was involved in a project rescuing a strain of Spanish pigs left on an island off the coast of Georgia called the Ossobaw. We visited two farmers who were raising these hogs on acorns and peanuts to follow in the footsteps of the Spanish Iberico producers, creating a fat content high in oleic acids and much healthier for the consumer. The meat was sweet and delicious. We began working with these farmers to cure this meat with great results.

Then one day, everything went sideways. It was in the spring of 2006. The health inspector made an unannounced visit to il Buco and our unsanctioned salumi facility downstairs. Though we were as rigorous as we could be, obviously we were not up to code. Bernardo had meticulously followed safety guidelines to ensure that his salumi had the proper pH and water content, but we had not filed an HACCP plan—the small mountain of paperwork that we would have needed to complete to be legit. At the time, and even now, salumi and the health department eye each other warily. What's more, salumiere necessarily introduce bacteria to their protein and let it flourish in order to properly cure the meat in the absence of traditional cooking methods. Nothing could be more abhorrent in the risk-averse black-and-white eyes of the law.

When Bernardo reported the next morning for work, he came across a massive pile of his beloved

prosciutto and salumi on the curb of Bond Street. At first he thought it was a terrible mistake, that perhaps someone mistook these darkened shapes for trash. He rushed to rescue them. But upon approaching the pile, he smelled the piercing aroma of bleach. The inspectors had instructed our staff to cut up the meat and douse it in bleach to render it inedible. This pile represented for Bernardo not just years of work and experimentation at il Buco but also the dream that a kid from Puebla, Mexico, could through the sheer force of work and drive become a legitimate Italian salumiere in New York City. He was, of course, heartbroken.

Losing the prosciutto and the rest of the salumi that morning, and seeing how hard hit Bernardo was, I vowed to one day find a way to restore our wonderful salumi program legitimately. This was one of the primary motivations for opening Alimentari. It would be six years and many misses before we happened upon the lumberyard on Great Jones Street. But this time, I resolved we would do it right. We would follow every rule to the T.

But we needed help, someone who was a professional salumiere. So I called Christopher Lee, who had worked with my friend Alice Waters at Chez Panisse for sixteen years. Chris was the one who started their meat-curing program. He was living in Berkeley at the time. The challenge of restarting a salumi program, and the possibility of building it literally from the ground up, was appealing to him. He brought us a sample of his own home-cured prosciutto and we were immediately sold.

Chris showed up with an enormous amount of patience, detailed knowledge of bureaucracy, and a folio full of recipes. He was one of the first salumi masters in the United States and had frequently traveled to Italy to learn from the masters there, like Francois Vecchio and Dario Cecchini. Over time, he and Bernardo worked together to standardize and professionalize the program at il Buco and planned for what they would build at Alimentari. State of the

LEFT: Bernardo processing a pig FOLLOWING, CLOCKWISE FROM TOP LEFT: Pig delivery; pig from Flying Pigs Farm; hanging house-cured salumi; tying off the porchetta; Alimentari Chef Preston Madson; salumi platter, il Buco Alimentari; Mike Yezzi, Flying Pigs Farm

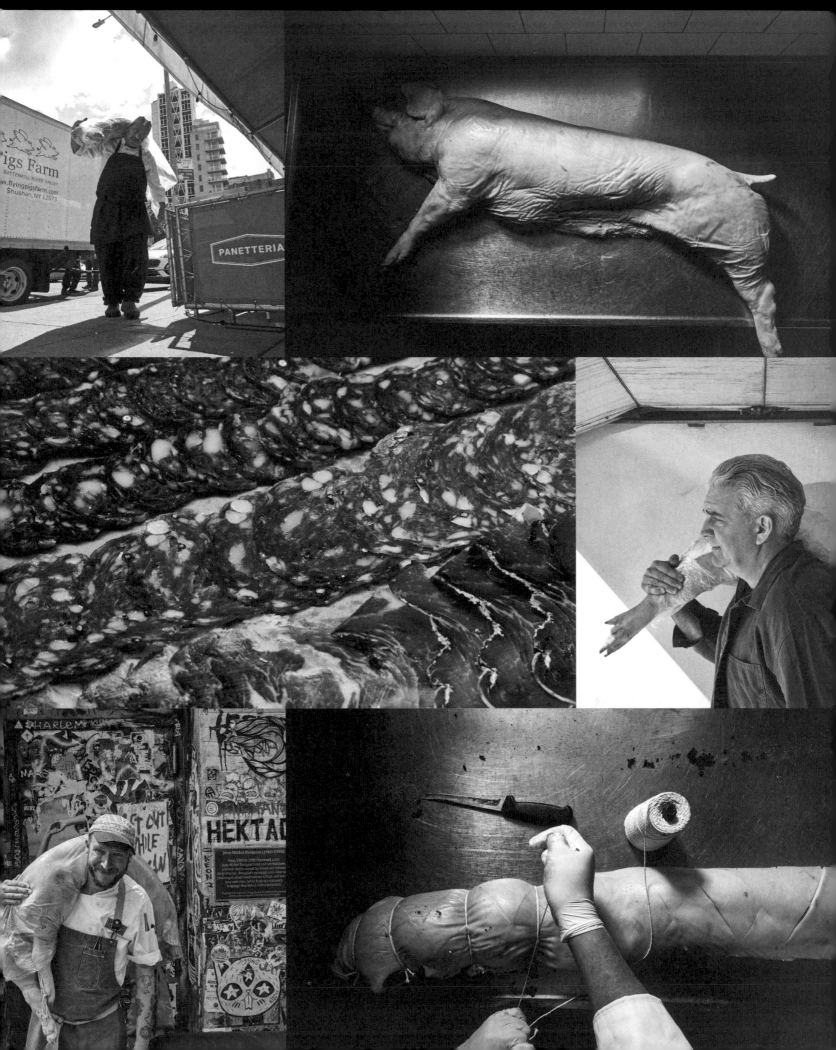

art curing boxes were brought in from Umbria under Alberto's guidance, and the space was taking shape.

Because it was so central an element to our project, I was adamant that we open with salumi already made. This, of course, presented a whole range of logistical challenges for the team. A prosciutto, for instance, takes a minimum of fourteen months of aging. Fourteen months before we opened il Buco Alimentari, it was still very much a construction site. Luckily, Chris convinced his friend Bev Eggleston in Virginia to "host" some of our early efforts. As we got closer to opening, Chris and Bernardo spent day and night breaking down hogs and turning them into various salumi and salame. Inside a pristine butchering room, they worked in almost balletic harmony, deftly wielding their knives and wasting nothing. They carefully weighed and salted the muscles to what would become the whole muscle cuts. They added the herbs and mixed what would eventually become sausage. Then onto a rack and into a quiet dark room the meat went, to age for months to come. When we finally opened our doors in September, not only was I proud to have our own salumi in the case, but I was happy to know that in our basement there was a completely HACCP-certified facility, full of aging salumi.

Chris helmed the opening of the market and worked hand in hand with Bernardo until 2013 when he returned to California, leaving Bernardo to lead our program. The salumi received accolades from clients and friends in the industry alike from day one and has been the highlight of the market. The salumi plate is still one of the most popular things on the menu at both il Buco and at Alimentari. Bernardo, meanwhile, has grown too. His kids, babies when I first met them, have grown up and gone on to college. (His son graduated with a degree in criminal justice. His daughter is a pediatrician.) His nephews and extended Flores family members—Angel, Pancho, Marcelo—have been working with him for years at il Buco, each lending his craft and dedication to our team. Over the years, Bernardo has truly become a master salumiere.

Often, on my frequent trips to Italy, the birthplace of salumi, I'll find myself missing Bernardo's salumi on Great Jones Street and the deep sense of nourishment I get every time I walk into Alimentari.

LEFT: Angel, Bernardo, and Marcelo Flores

BRANZINO AL SALE

———

I think the greatest expression of a piece of fish is to be cooked under salt—it's in its natural environment. The salt crust preserves the moisture of the fish and it allows the slow osmosis of salt into the skin. It's one of those techniques that's so simple and brilliant: the end result has perfect texture and delicate flavor.

Each time I have it, cracking open the crust, I feel the same joy as when opening a package, the same kind of wonder at how delicious it is, as if I hadn't had it a million times. At home I use fiore di sale—it's indulgent but well worth it; coarse sea salt is more commonly used.

....

Serves 4

4 (1-pound) whole branzini, cleaned
½ teaspoon fine sea salt
Freshly ground black pepper to taste
4 sprigs parsley
4 large sprigs thyme
4 sprigs rosemary
3 lemons, 1 sliced into rounds, 2 halved
2 tablespoons extra virgin olive oil, plus additional
    for garnish
1 large egg white at room temperature (if using
    coarse sea salt)
2 tablespoons whole pink peppercorns
4 cups coarse sea salt or fiore di sale

1. Rinse the branzino and pat dry. Place the fish on a large platter and season with fine sea salt and black pepper, making sure the fish are well coated, inside and out. Fill the cavity of each fish with a selection of parsley, thyme, and rosemary sprigs and a couple lemon slices. Drizzle lightly with 2 tablespoons of olive oil.

2. When ready to cook, preheat the oven to 400°F. Place the fish on a parchment-lined sheet pan.

3. Whisk the egg white until frothy, then gently fold in the pink peppercorns and coarse sea salt. The consistency should be akin to wet sand. (If using fiore di sale, egg white will not be necessary.) Spread the salt mixture over and underneath the fish, packing it tightly over the tops and sides so that the fish are fully enclosed. Place 2 halved lemons next to them, cut sides up.

4. Roast until the salt crust turns golden brown, 30 to 35 minutes.

5. To serve, plate individually with a roasted half lemon with each fish. Let your guests break the crust (which shouldn't be eaten) to reveal the treasure inside. Offer a drizzle of olive oil to garnish.

"We'll never forget the warm, cozy, and laid-back atmosphere in the room when we walked in with our newborn. The sense of homecoming and indulgence was the most comforting celebration of new life possible."

—INEZ VAN LAMSWEERDE
& VINOODH MATADIN

FISH IN ACQUAPAZZA

Fish in acquapazza is one of those perfect combinations of circumstance and flavor that restore your faith in the world. According to Italian culinary lore, the preparation of poaching a fish in seawater came from poor Neapolitan fishermen: why waste money paying for salt when the sea from which you caught the fish is full of it? But it wasn't until the 1960s, when the famous Italian comedian Toto popularized it by requesting it from his favorite restaurants in Capri, that it became widely available. The first time I had fish in acquapazza was in Vigo, a town by the seaside in western Galicia, just above Portugal. This time it was turbot, so succulent and juicy, with thin sliced potatoes perfectly tender. When I found out how easy it was to make, I was amazed. I've made it ever since when I host dinner parties for my closest friends.

Serves 4 to 6

3 (1¼-pound) whole black bass,* cleaned

2 tablespoons sea salt, divided, plus more to taste

Freshly ground black pepper to taste

1 small fennel bulb, cut into thin wedges,
      plus fronds and stems

1 bunch thyme

1 bunch oregano

½ bunch parsley leaves

2 bay leaves, broken

1 lemon, sliced

½ pound red potatoes (about 2 to 3 medium),
      sliced into ¼-inch slices

2 large plum tomatoes, halved lengthwise

1 small onion, trimmed and quartered but with
      the root still attached

3 garlic cloves, smashed and peeled

2 to 3 sprigs anise hyssop (optional)

¼ cup extra virgin olive oil

Feel free to substitute branzino, turbot, or orata

1. Preheat the oven to 400°F.

2. Rinse and pat dry the fish. Season the fish with 1 tablespoon of sea salt and pepper inside and out. Gently stuff the cavity of each fish with the fennel fronds, thyme, oregano, parsley, and bay leaves, dividing equally among them. Add 2 slices of lemon to each cavity.

3. Gently place the stuffed fish in a large roasting pan. Surround the fish with potatoes, tomatoes, fennel wedges, onion, garlic, and anise hyssop, if using. Season with salt and pepper. Drizzle the olive oil across the fish and vegetables.

4. In a measuring cup, dissolve 1 tablespoon of sea salt in 1½ cups warm water then pour into a roasting pan. Cover the pan tightly with aluminum foil and roast covered for 15 minutes. Remove the foil and roast for additional 15 to 20 minutes, until the potatoes are tender and the fish is opaque and succulent. Using a spatula, move the fish to a cutting board.

5. Fillet the fish, leaving behind the bones and stuffing. Serve alongside the vegetables.

WILD ALASKAN SALMON ON CEDAR

The first time I met Francis Mallmann, the Argentinean master of fire cooking, was in 2004. Peter Kaminsky invited me out to lunch at Francis's house in East Quogue. We were seated at a beautiful wooden table with a huge fig tree growing through a hole in the center. All around us were planters filled with fresh herbs and on the table, beautiful wine in the finest stemware. Every moment is etched in my memory. One of the first things Francis served was a slow-cooked Alaskan king salmon. Succulent within, the fish was simple, elegant, and delicious.

Though we can't replicate Francis's handmade oven, this is our version of that wonderful dish. The cedar planks—also called cedar shingles and often available at hardware stores—give just the right amount of smokiness. This salmon goes perfectly with grilled spring onions.

Our friendship was born over this delicious meal and a few months later, it was Francis who introduced me to Ignacio Mattos. Some fifteen years later, through continued gatherings at each other's homes and restaurants, our bond endures.

Serves 4 to 6

1 (2-pound) wild Alaskan king salmon fillet
½ cup granulated sugar
1 cup coarse sea salt
1 cedar plank (be sure it is food grade)
Fine sea salt to taste
Freshly ground black pepper to taste
1 tablespoon extra virgin olive oil

1. Place the salmon in a nonreactive vessel and sprinkle with the sugar and coarse salt. Cover and let sit, refrigerated, for a minimum of 2 hours or overnight.

2. When ready to prepare, preheat the oven to 400°F. Soak the cedar plank in cold water for 20 to 30 minutes. Remove the salmon from the refrigerator, rinse to remove all the sugar and salt, and pat dry. Bring to room temperature.

3. Place the salmon, skin side up, on the plank. Sprinkle with the fine salt and pepper and brush with olive oil.

4. Place the plank on a sheet pan. Bake the fish until medium rare (between 110°F and 125°F), 10 to 15 minutes, depending on the thickness of the fillet. Alternatively, grill the salmon on the plank over medium heat for 15 minutes.

5. Portion onto plates and serve with grilled spring onions, ramps, or asparagus.

"Il Buco is where I took my wife on our first date. Luckily, after sitting next to my ex-girlfriend and having ten friends come in and interrupt us to say hello, she agreed to see me again. The rest is history."

—JOSH TUPPER

BACALAO PIL PIL

Pil pil means "shake shake" in Euzkadi, a Basque dialect, and the secret to this dish is the constant agitation of the fish in the olive oil. This allows the gelatin and fats of the fish skin to combine with the olive oil to form a delicious creamy emulsion. It's like an aioli without the egg. What's so beautiful to me about a pil pil is how simple its preparation is and yet how the alchemy of oil, garlic, and cod becomes something so complex and delicious.

For me, bacalao pil pil brings me back to my apartment, maybe ten years ago. I was still married to Luca, and his parents were in town for their fiftieth anniver-sary. Alberto was in town and wanted to make some-thing special for my in-laws. We were eating in the wine cellar of il Buco, but Alberto didn't want to disturb the il Buco kitchen, so he prepared the dish in a large terra-cotta dish called a cazuela upstairs in my apart-ment, running back and forth to the cellar. By the time he got to the agitation part of making bacalao pil pil he had had quite a few glasses of albariño. He pil pil-ed so much that more oil ended up on the kitchen floor than was left in the pan. Though the meal was a triumph, we all spent the night on our hands and knees cleaning up the oil. The lesson here? Don't drink and pil pil!

Serves 4

24 ounces dried bacalao loins (salt cod loins), skin on
1 cup extra virgin olive oil
3 garlic cloves, smashed
1 large peperoncino
1 bunch parsley, leaves torn

1. Rehydrate the bacalao by soaking it in a large pot of cold water for 16 to 24 hours. Change the water at least three times. The longer the fish stays submerged, the less salty it becomes. Once the fish is rehydrated, remove and pat dry. Using a paring knife, carefully remove the pin bones.

2. Heat the olive oil in a large terra-cotta casserole (cazuela) or a large heavy duty sauté pan on the stove over low heat.

3. Add the garlic and crushed peperoncino, stirring gently for approximately 1 minute. Gently add the cod loins, skin side down. Agitate the pan constantly for 5 minutes so the cod does not stick to the surface of the pan and the fish skin begins to release its gelatin into the olive oil. While agitating, add 1 teaspoon cold tap water drop by drop to trigger an emulsion. Continue agitating for another 5 to 10 minutes until the cod is opaque. Discard the garlic and peperoncino.

4. Serve immediately in the casserole, or plate and pour the emulsified oil mixture over the top of each portion, and garnish with parsley.

PORCHETTA ALLA ROMANA

All throughout Umbria, in the town squares and by the side of the road, you'll find porchetta trucks. One side of the truck will be open, revealing a counter and, usually, a man in a white apron behind it. Above or below the counter will be painted, in bright beautiful letters, three words: *Porchetta. Panini. Bibite*. Porchetta. Sandwiches. Drinks. The three most beautiful words in the Italian language. Most important, glistening beneath a pane of glass will be the porchetta itself, a golden crispy roasted pig, wafting a combination of fennel pollen, rosemary, and thyme.

Pigs, from the famed Chianina breed to the two-tone Cinta Sinese, are an important part of the Umbrian and Tuscan cuisines. Traditionally, porchetta is made either with a whole roasted baby pig—deboned, stuffed with garlic and herbs, sewn back up, and slowly roasted—or a *tronchetto di porchetta*, the same preparation but using just the trunk of a pig.

Crisp, succulent, fragrant, hearty, there's no reason porchetta shouldn't be an American staple. The porchetta first made its appearance at il Buco with Sara Jenkins, who had grown up in Italy, where she had developed a deft hand with roasting meat. But today, preparing the porchetta falls to Bernardo Flores. This recipe for the home cook, rather than using a whole suckling pig, is based on what Bernardo makes at home for his wife and kids. So he uses a deboned skin-on pork shoulder, and instead of a rotisserie, he uses his oven. The secrets to getting the Holy Grail of porchetta—a crisp outside and juicy, fragrant inside—are the same. It is essential to create a uniform thickness to the meat, so take the time to trim the thick parts and place those bits where the shoulder is thinner before rolling the porchetta to ensure even cooking. Also, before you cook it, the rolled and tied porchetta needs to sit refrigerated for at least twenty-four hours and up to five days so that the surface dries out.

Sliced thick, the porchetta makes a wonderful main course. Sliced thin and served on a rosetta (or any sort of round roll) with arugula and salsa verde, it makes perhaps the perfect sandwich. So if you're feeding a smaller group, use the leftovers from this recipe for your panini the next day. *(Continued)*

PORCHETTA ALLA ROMANA

Serves 8

6 garlic cloves
4 tablespoons fennel pollen
2 tablespoons ground fennel seeds
4 tablespoons fresh sage leaves
4 tablespoons fresh rosemary leaves
4 tablespoons fresh thyme leaves
4 tablespoons fresh oregano leaves
4 tablespoons fine sea salt, divided,
    plus additional to taste
2 tablespoons lard, melted
8 pounds boneless skin-on pork shoulder,
    butterflied, trimmed to ½- to ¾-inch thick
8 (14-inch) pieces of butcher twine
2 tablespoons extra virgin olive oil
Freshly ground black pepper

"Once I took Donna to meet some Ossabaw pigs I had bought in the Carolinas. Long story short, she brought a few of them back to New York along with two salumiere from Umbria to begin the salumi program. Six months later we cut into our first ham. As soon as I tasted it, I immediately called Bryan Miller and Daniel Boulud to hop a cab downtown and try some. They damn near licked their plates clean."

—PETER KAMINSKY

1. Combine the garlic, fennel pollen, fennel seed, sage, rosemary, thyme, oregano, and 2 tablespoons salt in a food processor. Blend for about 2 minutes until finely chopped. Stream in the melted lard and pulse until combined.

2. To prepare the porchetta, lay the shoulder flat on the work surface, skin side up. Score the skin with a sharp knife, taking care to cut through the skin but not into the layer of fat underneath it. Flip the shoulder over. Carefully trim the thick parts, moving the scraps to areas where the meat is thinner, until the thickness is uniform, between ½ and ¾ inch thick.

3. Arrange the lengths of butcher twine on your work surface so that they are parallel to each other and about 1½ inches apart. Place the shoulder over the twine skin side down.

4. Season the exposed pork generously with the remaining 2 tablespoons salt, then cover with an even layer of the porchetta seasoning, massaging into the meat. Starting from one of the long sides, roll the pork into a tight spiral and and tie it tightly with the butcher twine. Transfer to a baking pan and refrigerate, uncovered, for 24 hours or up to 5 days.

5. When ready to cook, preheat the oven to 500°F. Let the porchetta come to room temperature. Rub the skin with the olive oil and season with salt and pepper.

6. Roast in the center of the oven for 25 to 30 minutes, then reduce the heat to 325°F and let cook for an additional 50 to 60 minutes, or until the internal temperature reads 145°F. Let rest at room temperature for 30 minutes.

7. Remove the twine. Serve sliced thickly as an entrée or sliced thinly on a sandwich roll with arugula and salsa verde.

ROASTED CHICKEN

My point of reference for roasted chicken is Angelo Scolastra, Alberto's mentor and the father of Luisa. In the early days of Villa Roncalli, a beautiful inn in Foligno, Angelo oversaw the kitchen and served guests in a beautiful dining room. In his later years, with his wife, then daughter at the helm, Angelo retreated to his rustic outdoor kitchen. If you were his friend, you were invited to eat there, where he'd bring whatever he had found in his *orto*, or garden, and effortlessly throw together the best dinner you've ever had. One memorable night, the dinner included a simple roasted chicken. Angelo had rubbed the skin with homemade lardo so that by the time it emerged from the oven, the chicken was golden and crisp. Inside, the garlic and rosemary imparted their intense flavor into the meat, and the best lardo-drizzled roasted potatoes blew your mind.

As a restaurateur and not a chef, I realize that part of il Buco's success relies on my being able to be open to the interests, tastes, and memories of my chefs. This recipe, for instance, comes from Preston Madson. Tall and heavily tattooed, with a Georgian drawl and a predilection for the Grateful Dead, Preston brings his own flavors to the table. Not unlike Justin Smillie, who first introduced me to Preston, he has a predilection for the Japanese pantry: from *katsuobushi*, dried fermented tuna that he flakes with miso butter into a roasted sweet potato; to *shio koji*, a mixture of malted rice, salt, and water, which he uses here as a marinade to add depth of flavor to the chicken. It might not be Italian, but I can't argue with the result: a golden umami-rich bird as delicious as anything I had at Angelo's table.

Serves 4

1½ cups shio koji
1 tablespoon chopped fresh oregano
1 tablespoon chopped fresh rosemary
1 tablespoon chopped fresh sage
2 garlic cloves, chopped
1 (4- to 4½-pound) chicken
Fine sea salt to taste

1. In a blender, combine the shio koji, oregano, rosemary, sage, and garlic and process until smooth.

2. Rinse the chicken, then dry it inside and out. Place it in a large bowl and slather it with the shio koji mixture, making sure it is well coated inside and out, sliding fingers under the skin to loosen and spread under the skin as well. Place the chicken in the refrigerator to marinate overnight.

3. When ready to cook, preheat the oven to 300°F. Remove the chicken from the refrigerator and allow to come to room temperature.

4. Place the chicken in a roasting pan in the oven and roast for approximately 60 minutes, basting occasionally with natural juices. Raise the temperature to 425°F and continue cooking for 15 minutes without basting until the skin is golden and taut and the internal temperature reaches 165°F or until the juices run clear.

5. Remove the chicken from the oven and let rest 10 to 15 minutes. Serve, sprinkled with salt to taste.

PEPPERCORN-CRUSTED RIBEYE

Most people don't think of steak when they think of il Buco. Yet if you've ever eaten the steak on Bond Street, you might quickly become a convert. Once again, the prime materials sing. We use the grassfed antibiotic- and GMO-free ribeye from Painted Hills Farm in Fossil, Oregon. The secret to this dish is the profusion of peppercorns, pressed hard into the meat and left there so they impart their flavor in the grilling process and form a delectable crust. The arugula meanwhile adds a sharp bolt of vegetal spiciness, and the little bit of smoked salt to finish both intensifies the meat and adds a surprising depth of flavor. And don't forget a drizzle of the best olive oil you can find over the thin slices of meat; I highly recommend the Umbrian Moraiolo.

Serves 4

1 ounce whole black peppercorns
1 ounce whole white peppercorns
1 ounce whole green peppercorns
1 ounce whole red peppercorns
1 cinnamon stick (or 2 teaspoons ground cinnamon)
1 (45-ounce) bone-in ribeye
2 tablespoons plus ½ teaspoon fine sea salt, divided
¼ cup plus 2 tablespoons extra virgin olive oil, divided
3½ ounces arugula (about 4½ cups)
Juice of 1 lemon
1½ teaspoons smoked sea salt
2 ounces shaved Parmigiano-Reggiano cheese (about ¼ cup)

1. Combine the peppercorns and cinnamon in a mortar and pestle or spice grinder. Grind until coarse.

2. Evenly spread the peppercorn mixture on a sheet pan. Press the steak onto it, making sure the peppercorns adhere and that each side is well coated. Let the steak rest at room temperature for 1 hour.

3. Meanwhile, preheat the oven to 350°F.

4. When ready to prepare the steak, evenly sprinkle it with 2 tablespoons of salt. Heat 2 tablespoons of the olive oil in a large cast iron skillet over medium-high heat until shimmering. Add the steak, using tongs to press it down. Sear the steak, turning once, until a dark crust forms, about 5 minutes on each side. Holding the steak with tongs, cook it for a minute on each edge as well.

5. Transfer the skillet to the oven. Cook the steak, turning it once after 10 minutes, until it reaches an internal temperature of 125°F (for medium rare), about 25 minutes total.

6. Meanwhile, prepare the salad by tossing the arugula together with the ¼ cup of olive oil and lemon juice in a bowl. Sprinkle with ½ teaspoon sea salt.

7. Remove the steak from the oven and place on a cutting board. Let the meat rest for 5 minutes on one side, 5 minutes on the opposite side, allowing the heat from the bone to further cook the meat.

8. To serve, slice the meat against the grain into ¼-inch-thick slices. Fan it out on a large cutting board, sprinkling a line of smoked salt on the side. Top sliced meat with arugula salad and finish with shaved Parmigiano-Reggiano cheese.

"I dream about the steak and that kale salad...and tuna on white beans, and the olive oil, and wine, and great conversation!"

—SOFIA COPPOLA

SHORT RIB WITH HORSERADISH

This gargantuan piece of roasted beef, served on a wooden board overflowing with strips of celery, walnuts, and Castelvetrano olives and finished off with that elixir of pure anchovy juice—colatura—always brought to mind one of my all-time favorite TV shows. It would clearly have been a Fred Flintstone favorite, a caveman's delight in any era. Fitting, since when Justin Smillie and I started Alimentari my pet name for the 6'4" chef was Bam Bam, with his tuft of blond hair above his cherubic face. Working with him was always entertaining, and I almost always ate too much. With a dish as delicious as this, who wouldn't?

....

Serves 4

For the brine
½ cup coarse sea salt
2 tablespoons honey
1 whole lemon, sliced
1 garlic clove
½ red onion
4 sprigs parsley
4 sprigs thyme
2 bay leaves
1 tablespoon whole black peppercorns

For the roast
2 (6- to 8-pound) whole, center cut short ribs
2 ounces black peppercorns, coarsely ground
1 ounce white peppercorns, coarsely ground
1 ounce green peppercorns, coarsely ground
1 ounce red peppercorns, coarsely ground
5 tablespoons extra virgin olive oil

For the garnish
5 stalks celery, cut into 5-inch batons
A few parsley leaves
¼ cup toasted walnuts, lightly crushed
¼ cup pitted Castelvetrano olives
1 tablespoon lemon juice
1½ teaspoons extra virgin olive oil
1 teaspoon colatura, divided
Fine sea salt to taste
1 tablespoon freshly grated horseradish

1. Prepare the brine by boiling 2 quarts water with the coarse salt and honey, then stir in the remaining brine ingredients. Let cool. Submerge the short ribs in the cooled brine and refrigerate, covered, for 24 hours.

2. Remove the short ribs from brine and pat dry. Combine the peppercorns and spread on a half sheet pan. Coat the short ribs in the peppercorns by pressing down so that they adhere. Refrigerate overnight.

3. Preheat the oven to 350°F. Place the short rib in a roasting pan; bring to room temperature. Cover pan in aluminum foil and bake for 2¼ hours, or until tender. Let the meat rest, covered, for up to 1 hour.

4. Meanwhile, using a mandoline, shave celery batons into ribbons and put into ice cold water.

5. Preheat the oven to 400°F. Heat a large cast iron skillet over high heat, add 5 tablespoons olive oil, and sear the short ribs crust side down to caramelize, 4 minutes. Transfer to the oven and cook an additional 10 to 12 minutes. Rest on a cutting board for 10 minutes.

6. Pat the celery ribbons dry and mix in a bowl with the parsley leaves, walnuts, olives, lemon, 1½ teaspoons extra virgin olive oil, and ½ teaspoon colatura.

7. Carefully remove from the meat from bone and cut into 1-inch slices. To serve, fan out the slices on top of the bones on a cutting board, season with sea salt, top with the celery mixture, horseradish, and the remaining ½ teaspoon colatura, and serve.

LA VITA

———

One of the things I love most about Bond Street, where il Buco is located, is that in a city of avenues, it's short, and, in a city of speed, it's slow. Bond runs only the two blocks from Broadway to Bowery and for its entirety is made of uneven cobblestones first laid in the 1800s. You just can't speed across Bond, neither walking—especially in heels—nor driving. That sense of slowing down the rhythms of daily life is essential to il Buco.

Over the last twenty-five years, I've tried to make both il Buco and Alimentari embassies of *adagio*, a respite from the frantic tempo that marks the rest of life in New York City, even if my own life often speeds ahead at an overwhelming pace.

We've done this by creating a world well beyond the plate. It begins in Trapani, where wind and sun, not artificial heat, evaporate the water from the salt (pages 139–149), in the attic batterie of Daniela in Montegibbio (pages 167–177), and in the gentle pressing of Marco's oil in Foligno (pages 81–89). It is carried closer to these shores by our suppliers at Westwind Orchards in upstate New York, where Fabio Chizzola and Laura Ferrara raise apples, cherries, pears, and pawpaws, and by Nevia No at Bodhitree Farm in the New Jersey Pinelands, who faithfully tends her 65 acres completely chemically free. It's brought to Bond Street by Sheena's patient work in the downstairs bakery, allowing natural yeast to do its alchemical work in our dough, and by Bernardo, whose culatello and lonza hang for months in their carefully temperature- and humidity-controlled cave before they're ready to serve. Hopefully, the cumulative effect is that when you walk into il Buco, the pressing of time is lightened.

LEFT: Potter's wheel, Marche, Italy

You don't move in slow motion, exactly, but you do slow down.

That same sense of wanting to protect and preserve a slower, more mindful way of living is at the heart of Vita, our homeware line, everything from twisted beeswax candles to black terra-cotta cups and plates to linen aprons from Tuscany. Actually, Vita was always a part of the il Buco story. After all, we started off as an antiques store, reselling objects that themselves had been repositories of hours: old radios, tables whose wood had been worn by thousands of meals, quilts that stitched together communities. But we largely abandoned that aspect of the business when the restaurant side began to take off. It was simply too difficult to be serving tables and selling both the tables and chairs, let alone shopping for replacements! For Alberto, who always saw the restaurant as a means for supporting other enterprises, it was one of the reasons he stepped back from il Buco. And for me too, at heart a collector, it was a wrenching choice to make.

Happily, I had partners in crime in this new venture. In the early days of il Buco, Alberto introduced me to his Foligno chums, Antonello and Lorenzo Radi. The Radi boys, attached-at-the-hip cousins of the same age, were neighbors of Alberto, and my visits there were filled with time together.

Antonello, with his chiseled jaw, deeply tanned skin, and cerulean eyes, looks like he walked out of a Renaissance painting. In fact, his side of the family were the bankers and politicians. He did often help in the family business but is much more of a true Renaissance man, rising most mornings before dawn to work in his garden or paint vegetables and plants as the sun peeks over the horizon. A prolific painter, he creates brightly colored, boldly stroked oil paintings of tomatoes, anchovies, and radicchio that adorn the walls of Vita today. An avid collector of antiques and all things of beauty, he seems to know every artisan in Umbria by name and is referred to as a maximalist. Antonello's apartment, a sixteenth-century palazzo

in Foligno, a glorious mishmash of eighteenth-century ceramics, seventeenth-century Nativity scenes, sixteenth-century tables, Mongolian fur pillows, Persian ottomans, and Moroccan platters, has been featured in *Elle Décor*. The man can shop.

His cousin, Lorenzo, tall and fit, the slightly more serious of the two, is an architect who travels the world, building the interiors for Brunello Cucinelli. His father, Lanfranco, was a well-known architect and fine artist in Foligno, and Lorenzo clearly inherited his father's aesthetic refinement. His studio is beautifully set up downstairs in the family home, a treasury of antique collectibles blended with midcentury modern furnishings. His sense of style is unmistakable.

During the years of il Buco, they have become true dear friends of mine, and we passed many hours together in the streets and restaurants of Umbria or in the dining room of il Buco, plotting the day when we would create a line of beautiful artisanal goods to match the style of the restaurants. As we set about transforming the abandoned lumberyard that would become Alimentari, I immediately turned to the Radi boys for help. Lorenzo drew the first renderings for the space, and the two combed the antiques stores and markets of central Italy to find the beautiful elements that married Alimentari to the il Buco brand. Like Alberto, like me, they are fiercely attached to traditional methods of production, and everything they sourced hummed with an artisanal spirit. They saw the beauty in the imperfect. They, like me, agreed with the Victorian art critic John Ruskin, who wrote, "Imperfection is in some sort essential to all that we know of life. It is the sign of life in a mortal body. . . . Nothing that lives is, or can be, rigidly perfect; part of it is decaying, part nascent. . . . And in all things that live there are certain irregularities and deficiencies which are not only signs of life, but sources of beauty." Together we sought the handmade, the objects, both new and antique, crafted by artisans.

Antonello would unpack a terra-cotta plate from its crate with the same sort of infectious passion

with which Alberto opened a jar of Scalia anchovies. "Beautiful, Donna," he'd say, "the top. Top." It was time to bring the dream we shared of the artisanal home line to fruition. Time to bring some of the work of these wonderful Italian artisans to New York, for, as beautiful as their material was, many were still struggling small-business owners. That is, after all, the downside of slow living. And so, as I had done with Alberto years ago, I embarked on another series of journeys to Italy in search of artisans with Antonello and Lorenzo as my guides.

And so I find myself in Bevagna, where the temperature is 95°F, and the stones of the medieval buildings radiate heat. But inside the *cereria*, or candlemaker, an ancient storefront on a narrow side street, the thick walls and shade keep it cool. There, one of our artisans, a redheaded thirty-year-old named Marco, is standing above a wooden cauldron of liquid wax, wearing a leather apron. The vault-like store is lit only by candles—naturally—and by the natural light spilling through the open door. Pairs of candles connected by a joint wick hang on pegs. Hundreds more line the shelves. Reams of hemp for wicks and bars of beeswax—sunflower, nearly black and rare; mille fiore and acacia—wait to be melted. Honeybees buzz around, perhaps confused by how the fruits of their labor are being used.

Here Marco is making candles, the same way they've been made for hundreds of years. Steam rises from a vat of liquid wax, kept warm by a bain marie, above which a wheel with fifty-six pegs is suspended. From each peg hangs a hemp wick, and on each end, baby candles are forming. It takes twenty dips, more than three hours, for a basic candle. "If you don't have patience," says Marco "you don't become a candlemaker." Beeswax candles were once used by the nobles and very wealthy Bevagnese families to decorate altars and palazzi. (Everyday people used animal fat or tallow candles.) Now, they are sold only here and at il Buco. Marco himself learned the craft thanks to an educational program run by the town as part of the annual Mercato delle Gaite, a ten-day

festival during which hundreds of Bevagnesi don medieval clothing—white cotton coifs, jerkins, gowns, shifts—and hundreds of craftsmen, from jewelers to weavers to paper producers, open their doors. I had written it off as a Disney-like street fair until I actually experienced the Gaite about ten years ago. It was a mesmerizing spectacle, the full community participating in the rituals of the past, taverns open through the streets of this medieval village, the authentic costumes and performances distinctly tied to the past, preserved.

One hundred thirty kilometers to the west, in a small village in the Marche, Emanuele represents another Vita artisan, whose connection to the past runs in his blood. For 160 years, his family has been ceramicists. From their rustic studio just outside the city walls, Emanuele creates beautiful plates, cups, saucers, vases. There's a small bottega on the ground level where his pieces are sold. His workshop is on the second story, where he sits perched at a potter's wheel. Around him are hundreds of vessels in various stages of drying, readying for the kiln. The kiln itself occupies an adjacent room. Its walls are jet black from three centuries' worth of smoke. The white clay against the black walls, the red clay against Emanuele's tan hands, the sun through the lace curtains of a window; since 1792, little has changed.

Emanuele, a seventh-generation ceramicist, estimates he has made hundreds of thousands of pieces over the last twenty-one years. "Every piece is beautiful from the first piece I made to the last," he says proudly, as his well-practiced hand cups a lump of spinning clay. "Each is a step in my life." He presses the foot pedal, and as we watch, he drives his thumbs into the clay, forming a cup shape. Using one hand, buttressed against his thigh, he exerts pressure that in turn forces the clay upward. The cup turns into a bowl. "I played in this workshop as a child," he says. "I used to watch these movements before knowing what they were. So when I started at the shop, I wasn't learning as much as I was remembering."

CLOCKWISE FROM TOP LEFT: Burning double wick beeswax candle; tools of candlemaking; Joaquin twists a candle; more tools of candlemaking; twisted beeswax candle; Marco, candlemaker; drying candles; vat of melted beeswax FOLLOWING, CLOCKWISE FROM TOP LEFT: Emanuele in his studio; unglazed ceramic cups; potter's wheel detail; Antonello Radi; window in Emanuele's studio; Donna watches Emanuele at work; assorted glazed bowls; Lorenzo Radi; studio handprints

The bowl's shape begins to grow clearer. This bowl, large with straight sides, he explains, is an ancient shape his family has been making since the beginning. "They were used to collect the blood of pigs in January and February with which we made *sanguinaccio*," a type of blood pudding that is often sweet but is served in this region with onions. Antonello, who's with me, adds impishly, "They were used for everything from washing vegetables to washing the baby to washing up after sex."

Emanuele finishes the bowl and, using a wire, cuts it deftly from the wheel. He sets it gently on a shelf to dry, and we head downstairs to the shop. On the wall a hand-lettered sign reads: TERRA IMPASTATA CON L'ACQUA, ASCIUGATA CON ARIA E COTTA COL FUOCO. *(Earth mixed with water, dried with air and cooked with fire.)*

It's the definition of his craft, reminiscent of a similar sign that I saw in the Bertoni kitchen about balsamic vinegar. These definitions don't seem merely to define a product but a way of life, a sense of self. Emanuele flips open a photo album. Black-and-white photographs of his father, his uncle, his grandfather fill the pages. In image after image, they are bent over the wheel just as he was moments before and before them, from the wheel, emerge shapes similar to the one Emanuele just made. As I leave, Emanuele proudly shows me a mug from the shelf. It is slightly more perfectly imperfect than its neighbors. The lip is a bit uneven and the sides curve in and out. "My daughter made this," he says, happily. "She's the eighth generation."

In workshop after workshop all across Italy, I could repeat this story. From the blistering hot furnace there is the free-spirited glassblower Nadia just outside Rome, collecting the recyclable bottles and jars of neighbors far and wide in order to transform broken shards into magical forms, from glassware to lamps, to winged vases with breasts. She pulls the form from the melted matter according to whim or fancy in the small studio behind her home in the countryside where she lives with her partner, their young daughter,

and a myriad of dogs and cats. Outside Siena, Marta and Fabrizio craft their own colored glassware of more simple straightforward lines and continue to form ceramics as their father did before them. Traveling back across into Umbria, Carlo and his brother are working with Antonello and Lorenzo to design our black terra-cotta Assisi line with muted tones that carry the Italian patinas to New York City. Then there's the basement workshop in a small hamlet of Perugia of the terra-cotta master Antonio, whose simple white plateware I have lunched on for years in the enoteca Bottega d'Assu on the edge of my favorite square in Bevagna, where I had my own little townhouse on Vicolo Cinema 2. A few kilometers away the weavers in Montefalco still work tirelessly to make their quality linens of every color under the sun and the metal workers forge our iron candle holders as they have for centuries, while the marble craftsmen carve their mortars from precious stone that has survived the ages. The handwrought cutting boards too are honed by hand, some sanded fine, others showing off the age of the planks from which they were born.

The goods we bring to New York as part of Vita are not only objects to use on a table but are themselves the products of an entire approach to life. These are seen in the patinas on their surfaces, the unevenness of their forms, their very nature.

Vita has been part of a story created over time. It is as much a part of the people and the places as it is about the products. It is about my relationship with Alberto lasting more than twenty-six years, Roberto for twenty-three, and Antonello and Lorenzo, my fratelli Umbri, and all the producers and friends who are now a part of my extended Italian "family," and whom I have followed through all the turns and twists in their lives as they have in mine, from marriage, to loss, to the births of our children. It is the world my son was free to explore before he had words. It is the magic feeling you get when sitting across the table, sharing stories and ideas. That's why we call it Vita. Vita is life.

CLOCKWISE FROM TOP LEFT: Broken recycled glass for glassblowing; glass work in progress; Nadia's oven; Nadia at work; finished glass pieces; handblown glass tumbler in progress FOLLOWING: Assorted dishware from Vita's Assisi line

CONTORNI

FRIED POLENTA

This is my mother's favorite dish at Alimentari. She lives in Florida and never comes to New York without having it. We use rustic polenta integrale from Anson Mills, a wonderful company based in South Carolina. Glenn Roberts, the founder, is maniacal about finding heritage corn and rice. This polenta uses a red Trentino flint corn, which was almost extinct in Italy until a few years ago. It gives the polenta a lovely mineral flavor.

I've always loved the creamy comfort of polenta, but when Justin first served me this version—in which the polenta is rolled in more polenta, then deep-fried into wonderfully crispy squares—it was a revelation. Though I would, and do, eat this year-round, there's nothing better than a few squares of fried polenta with a roasted chicken (page 228) on a cold fall or winter night.

Serves 4

3½ cups Anson Mills fine yellow polenta, divided
1⅛ teaspoons fine sea salt, plus additional
    for finishing
¾ cup grated Parmigiano-Reggiano, divided
Peanut oil, for frying
1 teaspoon freshly ground black pepper

1. Whisk together 6 cups of water, 1½ cups of the polenta, and the salt in a large heavy-bottomed pot. Bring to a simmer over medium-high heat, whisking constantly until the polenta becomes slightly starchy, approximately 6 to 8 minutes. Reduce heat to low, partially cover, and cook for another 45 minutes, stirring often, until the polenta is soft. If the polenta cooks too quickly, add ¼ cup of boiling water to thin it out. Whisk in ½ cup of the Parmigiano-Reggiano cheese.

2. Turn the polenta out onto a parchment paper–lined sheet pan, cover with plastic wrap, and let cool, refrigerated, approximately 4 hours or overnight.

3. When completely cool, run an offset spatula along the four sides of the polenta to loosen it from the sheet pan. Cover a work surface in parchment paper. Invert the sheet pan over the parchment paper to turn the polenta out.

4. Cut the polenta into 3-inch by 3-inch squares. Using a paper towel, pat all sides of the squares until dry.

5. Pour the remaining 2 cups raw polenta onto a clean sheet pan and spread out evenly.

6. Meanwhile, heat about 4 inches of the oil over medium heat in a dutch oven to 350°F.

7. Coat the squares in the raw polenta. Working in batches, fry the polenta squares in the oil for 5 minutes, until golden. Remove using a spider or slotted spoon and drain on a paper towel–lined sheet pan. Garnish with the pepper, a pinch of salt, and the remaining ¼ cup Parmigiano-Reggiano. Serve immediately.

ROASTED BABY CARROTS WITH CUMIN

The gorgeous colorful baby carrots get a perfect sidekick to balance their sweetness with the cumin-spiced yogurt. I usually add some Espelette for another counterpoint in this Moroccan-inspired recipe. Look for these multicolored varieties in your local farmers' market and be sure to taste one to be sure they're flavorful.

Serves 4

¾ cup plain whole milk Greek yogurt
1 teaspoon ground cumin
Espelette or Aleppo pepper to taste
Zest and juice of 1 lemon
1 tablespoon plus ½ teaspoon sea salt, divided
3 tablespoons extra virgin olive oil
1½ pounds baby carrots with greens trimmed

1. Preheat the oven to 400°F.

2. Prepare the yogurt sauce by whisking together the yogurt, cumin, Espelette pepper to taste, lemon zest and juice, and ½ teaspoon of salt.

3. Add the olive oil to a large oven-safe sauté pan over high heat. Add the carrots and season with 1 tablespoon of salt. Sauté for 5 minutes, until the carrots are glistening, then transfer the pan to the oven. Roast the carrots for 25 to 30 minutes, tossing occasionally, until tender and slightly caramelized.

4. To serve, spoon the yogurt sauce onto the plate and spread slightly, arrange the carrots on top, and serve immediately.

"We had to hold the door of il Buco open to carry our baby son in for many memorable dinners. Now he's opening the door for us. It's one of our favorite restaurants anywhere!"

—DAPHNA KASTNER & HARVEY KEITEL

BRUSSELS SPROUTS
WITH GUANCIALE

_____

Brussels sprouts and bacon is a combination that extends well beyond the Mediterranean. It's a staple at many holiday tables and for good reason. The chewy, salty yet somehow slightly sweet bite of the guanciale against the flaking caramelized brussels sprouts with their strong vegetal note is instantly comforting.

Serves 4

1 tablespoon extra virgin olive oil
¼ pound guanciale, cut into ¼-inch-thick lardons
2 pounds brussels sprouts, trimmed and halved
¼ teaspoon fine sea salt, plus additional for finishing
Freshly ground black pepper to taste

1. Preheat the oven to 400°F.

2. Heat the olive oil in an oven-safe skillet over medium heat until shimmering. Add the guanciale and cook until the edges start to brown, about 5 minutes.

3. Drain half the fat from the pan. Add the brussels sprouts to the skillet with the guanciale and toss to coat. Season with the salt and pepper.

4. Transfer the skillet to the oven and roast until sprouts are tender, about 20 minutes. Sprinkle with additional salt to taste and serve immediately.

TURNIPS WITH THEIR GREENS

Turnips are tricky for me. A relative of the radish family, they share that slightly peppery, crunchy sensation when raw, but tend to get a bit sweet when cooked, and when they're overcooked and mushy, I'm no longer interested. Seared, al dente, as they are in this recipe, they're still bright, a little peppery, with a pleasing snap that goes wonderfully with the charred greens on top. Also delicious on the grill with their greens and something slightly acidic—as simple as olive oil, lemon, salt, and pepper as in the recipe here, or with a hint of anchovy butter to add a little umami.

Serves 4

1¼ pounds baby Tokyo or Hakurei turnips, greens attached
2 tablespoons extra virgin olive oil, plus additional for finishing
1 teaspoon coarse sea salt, plus additional for finishing
Freshly ground black pepper
½ tablespoon lemon juice

1. Trim away any wilting bits of the turnip greens and slice the turnips in half from the bulb to the base of the greens, keeping the greens attached.

2. Add the olive oil to a large cast iron pan over medium-high heat. When the oil is shimmering, add the turnips cut side down, allowing the greens to hang over the edge of the pan for the first few minutes to avoid overcooking them. Season with the salt and a generous sprinkling of pepper. Cook over high heat, using tongs to turn once or twice, until the turnips are golden and slightly tender, about 8 to 10 minutes. Stir in the lemon juice, top with a sprinkle of sea salt and a drizzle of olive oil. Serve immediately.

"Il Buco changed how I felt about restaurants, from my first meal a month after they opened. The combination of perfectly simple dishes that let each ingredient sing a little song to you had me hooked."

—VICKI FREEMAN

BROCCOLINI WITH ANCHOVY & GARLIC

Though I'm not a big fan of American broccoli, broccolini—also called *broccoli di cicco*—is one of my favorite vegetables. The stems are more tender and flavorful than their American counterpart and the fleurettes are smaller, but overall is not as acidic and harsh as its cousin, broccoli rabe. Here, the al dente stems contrasting with the sweet and spicy fleurettes is perfect with my favorite accompanying anchovies, and the heat of the peperoncino adds the perfect finishing note.

Serves 4

2 tablespoons extra virgin olive oil
1 pound broccolini, trimmed
½ tablespoon coarse sea salt,
     plus additional for finishing
4 to 5 anchovy fillets, packed in olive oil
     (preferably Sicilian)
1 garlic clove, finely minced
1 peperoncino, crumbled, or to taste
Freshly ground black pepper
1 tablespoon lemon juice

1. Add the olive oil to a large sauté pan over medium heat and heat until the oil is shimmering. Add the broccolini to the pan and season with ½ tablespoon of salt. Sauté, tossing to coat well in the oil, until the broccolini is bright and glossy, about 4 minutes.

2. Stir in the whole anchovies, garlic, and the peperoncino to taste. Continue sautéing until the broccolini is just tender but still al dente, 6 to 8 minutes more.

3. Season with salt and pepper to taste and the lemon juice. Serve immediately.

XVI

HOME

———

My father, Gerald Lennard, was a successful businessman. Originally trained as an accountant like his father, he quickly decided number crunching wasn't for him. He set off to work for one of their clients in the metals business and loved it. In 1962, he split off on his own to found Gerald Metals, his namesake metals trading company. He pushed himself relentlessly and became an innovator in the field.

He was a generous supporter of the arts both philanthropically and as a collector, a pursuit in which he deployed both his highly refined sense of taste and his flinty business acumen. The walls of his home were filled with paintings by artists he identified early in their careers and who also found their way to success. I think it gave him great pride to have his keen aesthetic eye validated.

Some of the art was displayed in his lovely home in Wainscott, a beach town on Long Island, a beautiful sun-flooded house with the sound of the ocean in the distance. The family used to gather on the porch out back facing Wainscott Pond, Dad's peaceful place.

I spent a lot of time there, as the ocean is also my place of peace; plus my restaurateur schedule made braving the Long Island Expressway much easier in the off hours. I would show up with Joaquin on a Friday afternoon and enjoy the tranquility away from the restaurant and the city. My relationship with my dad was not an easy one. Two Tauruses, our horns often clashed. But we were also similar in many ways: a love of nature and the ocean, art, travel, delicious food and wine, and a stubborn commitment to getting the details right.

My dad passed away in 2018 just before his eighty-eighth birthday, three months before Joaquin's bar

LEFT: Donna sets her table, East Hampton, New York

mitzvah. Joaquin chose to move the location of the event to his grandfather's beach house, where friends and family gathered as I wrapped Joaquin in his grandpa's tallit. Dad was very much present on that perfect June day. The full il Buco team was there too, preparing a feast to top all feasts, uniting us all in a joyous celebration.

The house is now on the market, and the real estate agent has given the space what he might call an upgrade. The paintings I remembered have now been replaced by the sort of generic art one sees in lifestyle catalogs. My dad's love of patterns and color, once evident in the upholstery of the chairs, is now hidden under white slipcovers. It's beachy and modern and beautiful, but I miss my dad's spirit.

On a recent summer weekend, I was out at my own house, a little cottage in East Hampton's Springs facing Gardiner's Bay, to entertain some friends. I needed a few extra glass pitchers for margaritas, and, since the house hadn't yet sold, I drove over to my dad's place to pilfer the kitchen cabinets. I had been there before, of course, since he passed and steeled myself for its new look. But it is still such a shock to see all the life and all the materials that my father had amassed during his almost ninety years exist somewhere between gone and going. Happily, the kitchen had been left largely untouched. As I searched the cabinets, memories flooded back to me. Touched off by well-worn wooden utensils, by the skillets in which I had made him hundreds of breakfasts, I drifted into reverie. The happiest I'd seen my dad had been hunched over a breakfast of fried eggs generously covered in shaved bottarga, or his favorite dinner, a bowl of my pasta con le vongole, which I so enjoyed preparing for him in that sun-soaked, perfectly appointed kitchen.

I eventually chose three distinct pitchers, locked the door, and headed home to prepare for the feast. I ruminated on my father's life and, naturally, my own life's path. For twenty-five years, I've been maniacally devoted to provenance. I've spent decades sourcing product. I've passed more sleepless nights than I care to remember, endured screaming matches over fennel pollen (and the acidity of a balsamic and the phenolic compounds in olive oil and everything else), and set off on endless quixotic quests to rescue from the quickening of time the old ways of doing things. My travels took me around the Mediterranean as well as up and down the Eastern Seaboard. From this labor came il Buco, a place that—though I am biased, of course—feels truly magical to me. Like an air bubble or an embassy or dispatch from an altogether more romantic time, it miraculously endures through all of New York City's constant change. But what is the sum? After all, I know of course that my own house will end up like my father's: empty of me. I'm sure that just as 47 Bond Street was once an artist's studio, and 53 Great Jones was once a lumberyard, in the future, they will be once il Buco and once Alimentari. As for me, I started off il Buco as a young woman, a widow, aimless; my story hadn't yet been written. I'm no longer so young and am aware that this has perhaps been my life's work. After all, the Greeks called olive oil the elixir of life, but even olive oil won't save me from mortality. I am lost in thought as I pull into my house. Roberto is standing in the front yard. A copy of *Gazzetta dello Sport* is tucked underneath his arm; its bright pink newspaper stands out in the lush greenery. He's wearing his usual uniform: a black shirt and pants, khaki utility vest with a profusion of pockets, and a straw panama hat. He has the same dreamy yet watchful look he's had for the last twenty years. He waves his hand to greet me, and his eyes soften into a smile.

I climb out of the car and open the door to my home. Inside, the kitchen is already in a state of preparation. Friends from the city are coming, a few neighbors, a couple of new friends too. I am preparing a best-of menu for tonight's party, developed from years hosting dinner parties like these, smallish gatherings usually at dusk, overlooking some sunset, the more beautiful the better. The menu consists of low-impact

RIGHT: Accabonac Harbor, dusk

dishes that allow me the freedom to actually spend time with my guests. Like most recipes I love, they are exceedingly simple, relying on the quality of ingredients, not the complexity of the preparation. I slice the potatoes for the Fish in Acquapazza (page 219) and massage a dozen peppers with olive oil, pop my crostata in the oven (page 282), and head down to the bay. The temperature is perfect, and I dive in for a quick swim. The cool water is fresh and calming and my mind wanders: What is the sum of these past twenty-five years of il Buco?

The sun inches closer to the water, and the few clouds in the pink sky become edged with gold. Guests begin to arrive. Some I have known for years. Others I'm meeting for the first time. As they enter, with bottles of wine and bouquets of flowers, we hug and kiss. We head to the back porch for the margaritas with anise hyssop—thank God I found those pitchers—and a few cheeses I brought from il Buco's cave and some anchovies laid over a slather of Sheena's fresh churned butter on her buckwheat toast.

Though there is still much to do and much to grill, suddenly this house is full of bonhomie and ease. In a large bowl, cockles soak for the Pasta con le Vongole (page 188), and in another, the now-stuffed fish glisten. A stack of terra-cotta plates from Vita await deployment; a case of wineglasses wait to be filled. All of these goods look great in a showroom or in the display of Alimentari, but they look even better at home. This is, after all, where they're meant to be enjoyed.

Soon enough, it is time to sit down. I've sat at thousands of tables in my life, but each time—a new gathering, a new group of people, a new location—I still get a thrill of excitement at the sound of chairs scooting in, the clink of glasses against glasses, the amiable chatter before a feast begins. These moments are pregnant with expectation, these moments made even more precious for they are so fleeting. Yet, perhaps because I know this evening will last only a few hours, I try to let these moments flow through me.

I know if I try to hold on to them, I'll only grow as frustrated as my cat, Keiko, chasing rays of sunlight.

As the sun slips below the horizon, we light a few candles that I had watched Marco hand-dip in Bevagna. Small ramekins on the table hold salt from Massimo in Trapani, the hint of rose now coming out as the sky blazes brilliant pink. A cruet contains olive oil from the groves through which Marco Pandolfi and I walked, and in a narrow-necked glass bottle, balsamic vinegar from Daniela Bertoni whisks me back to Montegibbio. To my left stands Roberto, holding a bottle of vin gris from Rob and Maria Sinskey. The settings on the table before us were made by Carlo and Marta and a host of other artisans. From Bernardo's hand come the lonza and culatello, and from Sheena's oven come the loaves of filone she had baked earlier that day. Conversation flows easily and interweaves among friends. The words form a quilt of community. I don't know what we talk about, but I know we laugh a lot and the night flows lazily on.

Here in the dusk, I find my answer. Each element on the table is a totem for someone whom I've met through il Buco. Roberto, whom I adore and with whom I have spent most of my adult life; Alberto, the genius of il Buco whom I'll always love; all the artisans and farmers and producers, whose fates are intertwined with mine and whose land and labor provide the raw material for il Buco. I feel the table grow and grow so that those feasting around it include not just my friends in East Hampton on this one August night but friends and family and loved ones here and in Italy and Spain, those who are alive and those, like Joe and my dad, who aren't. They are present nonetheless.

I think of il Buco, the rich warm color of the wood and the soft yellow light that glints off the walls from the flickering candles and Warren's whimsical chandeliers. I remember countless nights returning home from a weekend out east or a trip across the ocean and walking through that door to find friends and neighbors and acquaintances gathered. Often they'd discover someone they knew across the room, from

CLOCKWISE FROM TOP LEFT: Guests gather by the water; Donna arranging flowers; Jill Platner, hand in hand; fairy eggplants in Lana Kova bowl; Roberto tends to wine; anise hyssop margarita FOLLOWING: Tablescape with Vita ware and Jill Platner napkin rings

another time or place or experience. Some are seated here with me right now. This makes me smile.

The truth is, I've never really considered myself a restaurateur. Il Buco happened in the most unusual, organic way out of the ashes of my past as a filmmaker and the loss of my life's partner. In short, I follow a life's quest for fulfilling experiences, formed from and forming relationships with people of various cultures and backgrounds, creatively moving through time and space. I surround myself with objects that bring me joy in their beauty and simplicity, often in their relationship to nature and to respecting her, and to the traditions of the past that endure in spite of the fast pace and evolution of industry. Each ingredient is chosen with respect for its authenticity and flavor and the connection to the people who created it.

That is what it has all been for. That is what it has always been for.

The sum total of my work and my life at il Buco is for this one effervescent moment, and now this moment is gone, and so it is for this one and this one and this one and this one and this one too. Ask anyone who's been to il Buco and they'll tell you, it isn't a place to go or a thing that can be held and therefore a thing that can be lost. It is a feeling, this feeling right now, in the flow of the present, the feast of this very moment.

"We started feeling at home at il Buco during the cold fall of 1994, going almost every night to dine, drink, and celebrate life. The familiar scent, the room full of friends, and that same old great feeling—a marriage for life."
—GUSTAVO TEN HOEVER

RIGHT: Dusk at home with friends **PREVIOUS, CLOCKWISE FROM TOP LEFT**: Donna, Roberto, Jill, and Scott, East Hampton; dress detail; spaghetti alle vongole; Donna and Joaquin; some favorite wines; Joshua David Stein; scallop ceviche; Lynda Stern and Scott VanderVoort; flowering chives; Keiko in her element

XVII

DOLCI

———

Panna Cotta with Aged Balsamic **274**

Ricotta Fritters **277**

Lemon Curd with Fresh Berries **278**

Olive Oil Cake **281**

Fresh Fruit Crostata **282**

Flourless Chocolate Cake **285**

Chocolate Budino **286**

Lemon Granita **288**

Blood Orange Sorbetto **289**

Salted Caramel Gelato **291**

PANNA COTTA
WITH AGED BALSAMIC

This rich yet strikingly easy-to-make dessert is mostly a vehicle for the delicate and delectable balsamic vinegar drizzled on top. This one's an Alberto creation, from the earliest days of working with our dear producer, Sante Bertoni. We use our own extravecchio from Sante's family at Acetaia Delizia Estense and fresh milk from Battenkill Valley Creamery in upstate New York.

Serves 6

2 sheets gelatin
½ cup whole milk
1½ cups heavy cream, divided
3 tablespoons granulated sugar
⅛ teaspoon kosher salt
⅓ whole vanilla bean, split
2 tablespoons aged balsamic vinegar,
    preferably at least ten years

1. Soak the gelatin in a small bowl of cold water until softened, about 5 to 10 minutes.

2. Meanwhile, whisk together the milk, 1 cup of the heavy cream, sugar, salt, and vanilla bean in a medium, heavy-bottomed saucepan and simmer until just shy of boiling.

3. Squeeze excess water from the gelatin and whisk into the hot milk mixture. Remove the pan from heat and strain through a chinois or a fine-mesh sieve into a bowl. Whisk in the rest of the heavy cream.

4. Divide the mixture among six ½-cup ramekins. Cover with plastic wrap and refrigerate 4 hours to set.

5. To serve, drizzle with high quality aged balsamic vinegar. Be as generous as you dare!

"Over 20 years, il Buco has introduced me to quail, fiore di zucca, morels, affogato, bomboloni, balsamic vinegar on panna cotta, and many many good friends."

—MICHAEL KLAWANS

RICOTTA FRITTERS

A cousin of the donut hole, a relative of the zeppole, this compulsively eatable dessert/snack showcases fresh ricotta's versatility. What other ingredient can you pair with blistered snap peas in a salad (page 58), with tomato and basil in a pasta, and then fry for dessert? I remember Sara Jenkins serving them first at il Buco with a lovely pomegranate molasses inspired by her time in Lebanon. Since then, they've become staples at our annual *sagre di maiale*, or pig roast (see page 293), but they're delicious year-round.

Makes approximately 20 fritters

1¾ cups fresh whole milk ricotta cheese
    (page 58), drained in cheesecloth overnight
¾ cup unbleached all-purpose flour
¼ cup apricot liqueur
4 large egg yolks
⅔ cup confectioners' sugar, plus more
    for sprinkling
Zest and juice of 1 lemon
⅛ teaspoon fine sea salt
Vegetable oil, for frying
¼ cup pomegranate molasses, preferably
    Al Wadi brand

1. In a small bowl stir together the ricotta, flour, and apricot liqueur. In a large bowl whisk the egg yolks, confectioners' sugar, 1 tablespoon lemon juice, lemon zest, and salt. Combine the ricotta mixture and egg mixture. Cover the batter and refrigerate for 15 minutes.

2. Preheat the oven to 325°F.

3. In a dutch oven, heat 2½ inches of the oil to 370°F over medium-high heat. Using an ice cream scoop or a large spoon, shape the dough into golf ball–size balls and carefully drop them directly into the oil, working in batches to make sure they do not touch. Fry each one until golden, turning so evenly browned, 6 to 8 minutes. Throughout, keep an eye on the oil to make sure the temperature stays steady and does not get too hot. Remove the fritters from the oil with a slotted spoon and transfer to a paper towel–lined plate to drain. Place the finished fritters on a rack on a sheet pan in the oven to keep warm while you make the rest.

4. When the entire batch is done, sprinkle with confectioners' sugar, drizzle with pomegranate molasses, and serve.

LEMON CURD WITH FRESH BERRIES

Who doesn't love the first strawberry of the season or mourn its passing? Yet, just in time, here come the raspberries and plump dark blackberries. Grab any of these luscious berries in season or anything of near equal quality and toss them over the top of a lemon curd made with Sicilian lemons. You'll have the most refreshing ending to almost any meal.

Serves 4 to 6

¾ cup freshly squeezed lemon juice, Sicilian
    if possible
1 cup granulated sugar, plus a bit more
    for sprinkling
Zest of 1 lemon
3 large eggs
2 large egg yolks
½ cup (1 stick) unsalted butter, cubed,
    room temperature
Kosher salt
1 cup cold heavy cream (optional)
2 cups seasonal ripe fresh berries, such as
    blueberries, raspberries, or blackberries

1. Place a pot filled halfway with water over medium heat and bring to a simmer. Set aside a medium heat-proof bowl that will rest on the edge of the pot, not touching the water below.

2. Whisk together the lemon juice, sugar, lemon zest, eggs, and egg yolks in the bowl. Place the bowl over the pot of simmering water and stir constantly with a wooden spoon or spatula. Be sure to scrape the bottom and sides as you're mixing.

3. When the curd is bubbling and thick and an instant-read thermometer inserted into it reads about 170°F, after about 6 minutes, remove the pot from the heat and stir in the butter and a pinch of salt until completely incorporated.

4. Pour the curd through a fine-mesh strainer into a large bowl. Place plastic wrap directly on top of the curd to keep a skin from forming. Refrigerate until chilled and set, 4 to 5 hours.

5. Meanwhile, if desired, in the bowl of a stand mixer, whip the heavy cream with the whisk attachment until soft peaks form. Alternatively, whip the cream in a bowl using a hand mixer or a whisk.

6. Sprinkle the fresh berries with a pinch of sugar and toss. To serve, spoon the lemon curd into small bowls or glasses and top with the berries and a dollop of unsweetened cream.

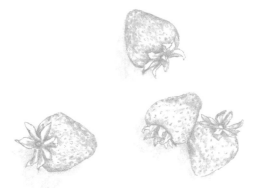

OLIVE OIL CAKE

It's amazing to me how much the simple substitution of olive oil for butter turns a pound cake I remember from my childhood, accompanied by a glass of milk, into an instant journey to Italy. Unbelievably moist with an intriguing sweetness, this cake has been on the menu of il Buco since the beginning. What I love about it, besides how well it showcases olive oil's versatility, is that olive oil is liquid at room temperature, so the cake remains moist much longer and, in fact, is sometimes even better the day after you bake it . . . if you can keep yourself from finishing it immediately out of the oven. Numerous simple toppings give it an extra flourish, but my favorite would be a handful of summer berries and a dollop of unsweetened cream or mascarpone.

Serves 6 to 8

1¾ cups granulated sugar
2 large eggs
5 large egg yolks
Zest of 1 lemon
½ teaspoon fine sea salt
1 cup extra virgin olive oil, plus more to grease pan
¾ cup cake flour
1 teaspoon baking soda
½ teaspoon baking powder
1¼ cups buttermilk
½ cup whole milk

1. Preheat the oven to 325°F.

2. In a stand mixer with a whisk attachment, combine the sugar, eggs, egg yolks, lemon zest, and salt at high speed until light and fluffy. On low speed, drizzle in the olive oil until incorporated.

3. In a separate bowl, whisk together the flour, baking soda, and baking powder until incorporated. In another bowl, combine the buttermilk and milk.

4. With the mixer on medium speed, alternate adding the milk and dry mixtures to the egg mixture—starting with the liquids—in two installments of each. Mix until a smooth batter forms.

5. Grease a large loaf pan with olive oil and pour in the batter in an even layer.

6. Bake in the center of the oven, rotating halfway through, until a skewer inserted in the center comes out clean, about 1 hour and 20 minutes.

"I've been going to il Buco for over 20 years, and almost every meeting I've had has been at those tables. But I love most my time alone at Alimentari in the mornings with the papers and my coffee."

—GABRIEL BYRNE

FRESH FRUIT CROSTATA

———

Cold butter is the key to a perfectly flaky crostata. And a perfectly flaky crostata is a wonderful way to end a leisurely meal. It's not too heavy or too sweet, and it is terrifically easy to make. (A crostata is, essentially, a half-made tart.) The traditional Italian version is made with *pasta frola* with a lattice top. This is a lighter, more buttery version, more akin to a French galette—please don't tell the Italians. In the summer, I'll visit one of the many farmstands out east, picking up pints of freshly picked blueberries or strawberries or stalks of rhubarb. But a crostata is a wildly accommodating dessert—pretty much any fruit will do as long as it isn't too liquidy. I like to finish mine with fresh whipped cream, but feel free to top with ice cream, preferably vanilla.

....

Makes 1 large crostata

1½ cups all-purpose flour
5½ tablespoons sugar, divided
⅜ teaspoon fine sea salt
6 tablespoons cold butter, cubed
3 tablespoons ice-cold water
4 cups ripe seasonal fruit, such as sliced
    strawberries (with or without sliced
    rhubarb), whole blueberries or
    blackberries, or a mixture of berries
Zest of 2 lemons
1 large egg
1 cup cold heavy cream (optional)
¼ teaspoon pure vanilla extract (optional)

1. Mix the flour, 3½ tablespoons sugar, and salt in a stand mixer with a paddle attachment for 30 seconds. Add the cold butter and mix on low speed until butter is in pea-size bits. (You do not want to form a solid dough at this point.) Add 3 tablespoons ice-cold water and continue to mix just until a shaggy dough forms, about 1 minute. Remove the dough from the bowl and pat together to make one uniform ball. Flatten into a disk, wrap in plastic, and chill for 2 hours, or up to 3 days.

2. When ready to bake, preheat the oven to 400°F.

3. Toss the fruit with 1 tablespoon sugar and the lemon zest and set aside to macerate while you roll out the dough. Break the egg into a small ramekin and use a fork to scramble for an egg wash.

4. On a lightly floured surface, roll out the chilled dough, working quickly so that the dough doesn't get too warm, into a circle about 16 inches in diameter and ⅛ inch thick. Place the dough onto a parchment paper–lined sheet pan. Spoon the macerated fruit evenly onto the center of the crostata round. Spread the fruit filling evenly over the dough, leaving 1 to 2 inches bare around the edges. Fold up the sides of the crostata (leaving the fruit uncovered in the center), pleating and pressing gently to seal as you go. Lightly brush the exposed edge with egg wash and sprinkle with the remaining tablespoon of sugar.

5. Bake for 20 minutes, then rotate the pan and cook for another 15 minutes until the filling is bubbling and the crust is golden. If the crust is getting too dark, cover with foil for the last minutes.

6. Meanwhile, if desired, in the bowl of a stand mixer, whip the heavy cream with the whisk attachment until soft peaks form; add the vanilla if you like and whip again for 30 seconds. Alternatively, whip the cream in a bowl using a hand mixer or a whisk.

7. Allow the crostata to cool and serve topped with whipped cream if desired.

FLOURLESS CHOCOLATE CAKE

I can't remember a time in the life of il Buco when we didn't have flourless chocolate cake on the menu. From the early days, I couldn't attend a family gathering without it. My nephew Mitchell Rubin, the true chocoholic in the family, waited expectantly for that cake when I arrived. Over the years, the recipe shifted, and my family always let me know when it had veered too far from the familiar path. This version, with its 64% chocolate, has been given the Mitchell seal of approval.

Serves 8 to 10

11 tablespoons unsalted butter, cubed,
    plus ½ tablespoon, softened
7 ounces 64% chocolate, chopped (about 2 cups)
1 tablespoon cocoa powder
2 tablespoons plus 1 teaspoon almond flour
5 large eggs
⅔ cup granulated sugar
1 tablespoon vanilla extract
¼ teaspoon fine sea salt
1 cup cold heavy cream (optional)
1 teaspoon confectioners' sugar

1. Preheat the oven to 325°F.

2. Add the cubed butter and chopped chocolate to a double boiler or a metal bowl set over a saucepan of simmering water over medium heat. Melt, stirring often, until smooth, about 5 minutes. Remove from heat and stir in the cocoa powder and almond flour. Set aside to cool.

3. In a stand mixer with a whisk attachment, whisk together the eggs, sugar, vanilla, and salt until it is thick and runs off the beaters in ribbons, about 6 minutes. Using a rubber spatula, gently fold the egg mixture into the chocolate mixture, taking care not to deflate the egg mixture.

4. Grease a 9-inch springform pan with the remaining ½ tablespoon softened butter and pour in the batter. Bake until the cake is set, about 30 minutes, then transfer to a wire rack to cool completely.

5. Meanwhile, if desired, in the bowl of a stand mixer, whip the heavy cream with the whisk attachment until soft peaks form. Alternatively, whip the cream in a bowl using a hand mixer or a whisk.

6. Sprinkle the cake with confectioners' sugar and serve with a dollop of unsweetened cream.

"I've had birthdays and baby showers and anniversaries and arguments and dates and meetings, all at il Buco over the past almost 20 years. It feels like home but on a special occasion."

—MAGGIE GYLLENHAAL

CHOCOLATE BUDINO

Slightly more sophisticated than the flourless chocolate cake (page 285) is the chocolate budino. Budino is, quite simply, Italian pudding. This version, topped with crème fraîche, is the perfect ending to a great meal. If you're a coffee fanatic, add the espresso powder for an additional kick.

Serves 6

2 cups whole milk

1½ cups heavy cream

¼ cup instant espresso powder (optional)

½ teaspoon fine sea salt

½ vanilla bean

1 cup plus 2 tablespoons granulated sugar, divided

5½ ounces 72% bittersweet chocolate, chopped into small chunks

6 large egg yolks

1. Preheat the oven to 350°F.

2. Add the milk, heavy cream, espresso powder (if using), and salt to a medium-size pot. Split the vanilla bean and scrape out the seeds, add both to the pot. Heat, stirring frequently with a wooden spoon, over medium heat until just shy of a boil, about 6 minutes. Remove from heat and discard the vanilla pod.

3. In a separate medium-size heavy-bottomed pot over low heat, heat ⅔ cup sugar, undisturbed, until it melts into a rich brown caramel, about 20 minutes. Remove from heat.

4. Slowly and carefully whisk the milk mixture into the caramel (mixture will bubble vigorously), whisking until incorporated. Reheat gently over medium-low heat and whisk until the caramel is dissolved, scraping up any caramel that has stuck to the bottom of the pot. Vigorously whisk in the chocolate, stirring until completely melted. Remove from the heat.

5. In a separate bowl, whisk together the egg yolks and remaining ⅓ cup plus 2 tablespoons sugar until incorporated. Slowly whisk 1 cup of the warm chocolate mixture into the eggs to temper them, then fold the tempered egg mixture back into the chocolate mixture. (If the mixture doesn't fully emulsify and you still see flecks of chocolate, you can strain it through a fine-mesh sieve, if desired.)

6. Create a bain marie: place 6 (6-ounce) porcelain ramekins in a large baking dish, then fill the dish with hot water until it comes about three-quarters up the sides of the ramekins.

7. Divide the mixture evenly among the ramekins in the bain marie. Cover the pan tightly with aluminum foil and cook until wobbly in the center but just set around the edges, about 1 hour and 15 minutes.

8. Remove from the oven, remove the ramekins carefully, and let cool on a sheet pan. Refrigerate until chilled and serve cold.

LEMON GRANITA

When I think of granita, I think of Trapani. I remember countless early morning rendezvous with Salvatore or Alberto Galluffo for breakfast in the Old Town. We'd sit outside our favorite spot, Collicchio, and alternate bites of warm brioche with ice-cold granita.

Granita, brioche, granita, brioche, granita, brioche. We'd repeat until the cup was empty. But this bracing and simple ice can also be used as a palate cleanser, if you want, or just as a bright grace note on which to end a summer meal.

Serves 4

½ cup granulated sugar
4 tablespoons freshly squeezed lemon juice
1 tablespoon lemon verbena leaves, finely chopped
2 cups seasonal ripe fresh berries

1. Combine 4 cups of water with the sugar, lemon juice, and lemon verbena leaves in a pot and bring to a boil. Allow to simmer 5 minutes.

2. Remove from the heat and let infuse for ½ hour. Then place into a wide, nonreactive container and freeze overnight.

3. To serve, scrape the frozen granita into individual bowls and top with the fresh berries.

BLOOD ORANGE SORBETTO

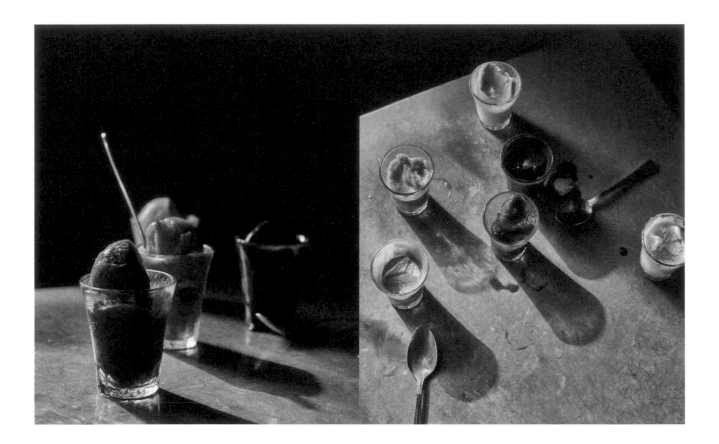

Deliciously tart and visually stunning, blood oranges were never part of my childhood growing up. But the first time I had them in Sicily, I was blown away. At il Buco Alimentari we make this delicious sorbetto with Sicilian blood oranges. It's sweet but tart enough to also function as a palate cleanser and so vibrant it refreshes the eyes as well.

Don't be put off by the strange ingredients in the list below. All are available online. Get adventurous and have fun—it will be worth it!

Serves 4

3½ ounces glucose syrup
½ teaspoon lemon juice
½ cup plus 3 tablespoons granulated sugar
1 teaspoon glucose powder
1 tablespoon plus 1 teaspoon sorbet stabilizer
7 ounces blood orange puree

Special equipment needed: ice cream maker

1. In a medium pot, bring 2 cups of water, the glucose syrup, and the lemon juice to a boil. Whisk in the sugar, glucose powder, and sorbet stabilizer.

2. Once the mixture has thickened, cool the pot in an ice bath. Whisk in the blood orange puree.

3. Follow the ice cream maker's instructions to process the gelato.

SALTED CARAMEL GELATO

Though no one can resist the siren call of a gelateria, I am not naturally inclined to finish my meal with anything but a strong espresso. Yet when Karen Sandoval, our first pastry chef at Alimentari, brought out a perfect scoop of this gelato, I was won over. She knew the way to my heart was the Trapanese sea salt she sprinkled on it. Partnered with the caramel, it's the perfect salty-sweet combination. Although it's a bit heretical, I love to plop a scoop of this in my espresso for a caramel affogato. (Traditionally, one uses vanilla gelato.) It's the best of both worlds.

....

Serves 4 to 6

6 cups whole milk
¾ cup heavy cream
1¾ cups granulated sugar
⅓ cup packed brown sugar
5 large egg yolks
2 large eggs
1 teaspoon fine sea salt
Fiore di sale to taste (optional)

Special equipment needed: ice cream maker

"You cannot have a pulse and leave il Buco without inspiration."
—CHRIS FISCHER

1. In a small pot, make the gelato base by combining the milk and heavy cream. Heat uncovered, stirring constantly, over medium heat until scalding but not boiling. Remove from heat.

2. To prepare the caramel, boil the granulated sugar and ¼ cup of water in a large heavy-bottomed pot. Cook without stirring until the mixture reduces to a very dark caramel color and is slightly smoky, with a thick but smooth consistency. Remove from heat.

3. Deglaze the caramel by carefully adding the still hot dairy mixture. Whisk in the brown sugar.

4. In a large bowl, whisk together the egg yolks and the eggs. Temper roughly a quarter of the milk-and-caramel mixture into the eggs by adding it in a slow steady pour, whisking constantly. (If the milk is too hot, the eggs will cook and form curds.) Slowly pour your tempered eggs back into the pot with the rest of the caramel and milk. While stirring constantly, heat the mixture over medium heat until it reaches 185°F.

5. Strain the mixture through a fine-mesh strainer into a large bowl. Cover and refrigerate overnight.

6. The next day, whisk the sea salt into the cooled gelato base. Follow the ice cream maker's instructions to process the gelato.

7. When serving, sprinkle a few crystals of fiore di sale on each portion if desired.

XVIII

FEAST

─────────

It begins the night before when a group of my guys—a rare joint exercise of the il Buco and Alimentari teams—builds a makeshift oven out of cinder blocks on the cobblestones of Bond Street. Working hand in hand, Preston and Roger, Olaf, Marcelo, Tiki, and Danny construct the oven in an hour or so, placing rebar atop, sturdy enough to support the three large pigs currently chilling in the walk-in refrigerator of il Buco.

The boys will be there all night long and well into the next day as they prepare a feast to feed hundreds. There's no question that the *sagra del maiale*, our annual feast of the pig, is a labor of love. In central Italy, a sagra is a community celebration usually centered on a selected ingredient coming into season, like asparagus or cordons, even truffles. We began throwing our sagra back in 2004, on our tenth anniversary, as a way to give back to our Bond Street neighbors, a community that has nurtured us and become our home. As the pig has been so revered at il Buco with our porchetta and salumi production, we chose to honor it in our celebration. On and off over the

years—but mostly on—we've hosted the event every September. This is the twenty-fifth-anniversary sagra.

This year, I'm lucky. Alberto has come over from Italy as have the Radi boys, Antonello and Lorenzo. Antonello, in fact, has offered to paint a side of the construction site adjacent to the restaurant, turning a flat of plywood into a bucolic scene of the Umbrian hills. I'm looking forward to the day, when all—or most—of our regulars and family and friends stop by to feast together.

Around 1 a.m., the fire glows in the night, illuminating the faces of the night crew. As waiters get off their shifts from both il Buco and Alimentari, they stop by

LEFT: Marcelo Flores, pig roast early morning, Bond Street, New York

for a drink: tequila, Peroni, wine. Olaf's friends, cops, stop by to say hi. He produces a few links of Polish sausages that are grilled on a flattop above the fire and passed around. Tranquilo. Tranquilo. At 2 a.m., it's time to get the pigs. Together the guys heft up our beautiful animals from my friend Mike Yezzi at Flying Pigs Farm in Shushan, New York. They place the pigs atop the rebar, carefully spreading the embers from the fire under their enormous frames.

I wake up in the early morning before sunrise, stumble downstairs, and join the boys by the smoky fire. Alberto, Antonello, and Lorenzo bring cups of espresso. I cook up some eggs in a cast iron pan on the grill; my yearly ritual to feed the team. The rentals arrive: tents, tables, tablecloths. We're expecting more than eight hundred guests. Marc and Lee Anne supervise the transformation of Bond Street into a vast outdoor dining room. Marcelo, meanwhile, tends to the pigs, using a mop dipped in brine to paint their skins. By now, they're developing a beautiful caramel skin. Smoke billows from the oven, rising up to the clear blue sky.

We have visitors all morning. Friends coming to check in, grab a coffee, and bask in the excitement. Neighbors taking their dogs for walks, kids atop their shoulders. Strangers intrigued by all the activity so early on a Sunday morning. The guys pull the first pig from the oven, the product of patience and Marcelo's tireless basting through the night.

By 12:30, the crowd starts to arrive. I am pulled in ten thousand directions, placing old faces, seeing friends, giving hugs and kisses. As I look around me, I'm overcome with gratitude for the community that has developed around il Buco. I see Bernardo Flores and his nephews, Marcelo, Angel, and Pancho. I see Sheena Otto, our head baker, with her daughter, Rita, now almost a year old. Harding Aldonzar, our tireless chef de cuisine, is commandeering the service. Even on a day as bright as this, his smile still shines. Roger wears the signature black il Buco T-shirt and tends to the meat next to Preston, tall and tattooed. I think

back to all the chefs who have passed through our kitchen, each indelibly imprinting themselves on the soul of il Buco. And then I spot Thierry Amezcua, our very first chef, arriving to join in the festivities, and the years contract instantly.

The regulars mill around, greeting one another and me. Simona and Andrea with their brood of daughters. Jill Platner's here. Scott and Lynda from across the street. Liev Schreiber and his son, Sasha. A bunch of former staff members I call Roberto's Girls: Patty and Dana and Carolyn, Abbie and Michelle. Roberto's there, of course, as steady and natural a presence as a breeze. He glides in and out of il Buco, wine bottle in hand, his straw hat keeping him cool. Gray is the hair that was once brown and long. And though his face bears more wrinkles than before, his eyes never cease to sparkle. Over the last twenty-five years, I've seen so many of il Buco's family grow, marry, have kids of their own. That il Buco had some small part in that—whether as a meeting place, or as a backdrop, as a memorable first date, or second or third—leaves me with a sense of almost maternal joy.

The day passes in a happy blur. Joaquin sitting with my mother at a table outside il Buco, friends reconnecting over wine and heaping plates of food. Life courses over the cobblestones of Bond Street. I find Alberto among the crowd, tipsy by this point, and give him a hug. As we said so many times before, but each time with incredulity, "We did it," I say. "*Si, cara,*" he replies, eyes twinkling.

As darkness falls, only the stragglers are left, coming into il Buco for a last glass of wine. Laughter continues well past dark, and I finally sit down to relax with a few dear friends as the crew sweeps up the ashes and dismantles and stacks the cinder blocks. I head upstairs, peel off my smoky clothes, and leave them in a pile on the floor. I drift off to sleep on a raft of happiness, grateful for all that brought me to il Buco, grateful for all those who have guided me on the journey, grateful to have passed yet another day surrounded by love and, of course, porchetta.

CLOCKWISE FROM TOP LEFT: Crispy skin; Alberto Avalle; fire detail; Antonello and Lorenzo Radi painting mural; Laura with baguettes; breakfast on the grill; Danny Rubin and Donna **FOLLOWING, CLOCKWISE FROM TOP LEFT:** Ricotta fritters; Michelle, Roberto and Carolyn; il Buco chairs; Chef Roger Martinez; Donna and Jill; Olaf; Tasha Cain; Joaquin and his dad, Alejandro; pig roast setup; Donna's sister Wendy and Danny; pig roast platter; Preston and sister Lauren Madson; il Buco crew; Emilio Mittidieri; head baker Sheena Otto with daughter, Rita; pork cracklings.

GRATITUDE

I owe an enormous amount of gratitude to my original partner in crime, Alberto Avalle, my dearest collaborator in all things il Buco, along with Roberto Paris, wine director extraordinaire, proverbial right hand, and padrino to my son, Joaquin, the light of my life. To my Fratelli Umbri and partners in Alimentari and Vita, Antonello and Lorenzo Radi, and to my own incredible family whose support buoys me daily. A special thanks to my dear nephew Danny Rubin, who has become a true member of the il Buco clan from prep cook to Alimentari director to leading the charge in Ibiza.

To all the chefs who have graced these spaces with their enormous talent and collaboration over the years: Thierry Amezcua, Jody Williams, Filippo Paoloni, Sara Jenkins, Amanda Freitag, Sandro Fioriti, Gary Robins, Ed DeWitt, Jeremy Griffiths, Anne Burrell, Ignacio Mattos, Christopher Lee, Justin Smillie (welcome back!!), Josh DeChellis, Joel Hough, Victoria Blamey, Roger Martinez, Garrison Price, and Preston Madson.

To the extraordinary Il Buco and Alimentari teams, with a special shout-out to il Buco kitchen veterans Harding, Tiki, Ricardo, and the Flores boys: Bernardo, Marcello, Angel, Pancho, Gabino, Isaias. To our amazing staff of servers, bartenders, and busboys and runners, to a rock star management team led by Marc Ellert-Beck and Natasha Riger. To David, Sheena, Lauren, Maya, Max, Jeff and Sherry, Boris and Alan, to my Vita girls Caroline and Giada, Fabio, Erica, Scott, and Rubyrose Hill; to Luca, Xavi, and the Bottega Ibiza team, and to Ari, Eric and Sharone, Cyril and Valerie, our sun-kissed Balearic coconspirators. To Anne Koczka, Tasha Cain, and Sofia Frias, who have cared for all the details over all the years, and to the original Banda del Buco cast, Giorgio Cappelletti and Carlo Pulixi. To Joe's loving family and his brother, Michael Rosato, whose artistic flourish has enhanced both restaurants since the beginning; and to Warren Muller, who brought in the light with his fantastical chandeliers.

To Alice Waters, Francis Mallmann, and Peter Kaminsky, whose friendships have inspired me. To Joshua David Stein, whose humor, poetry, and perception brought this story to life on the page; to Andrea Gentl and Marty Hyers, whose extraordinary photographs enhanced it, with the graceful assistance of Frankie Crichton. To Michael Grimm, Giada Paoloni, Thibault Jeansen, and Noe DeWitt for the beautiful archive of images over the years. To our dedicated stylists, Ayesha Patel and Susie Theodorou, whose attention to the details made all the difference, and to Su Barber, whose inimitable design tied together all the threads of this twenty-five-year journey. Working with you has been a dream. And thank you, Maya Horton,

LEFT: Donna and Alberto, Foligno, Italy (Gentl & Hyers) PREVIOUS: The il Buco family, 20th Anniversary Pig Roast PAGES 298-299: Donna paints the pig (Giada Paoloni); hoisting the pig, Mallmann style; Tiki and Anne; Donna and Georgio; Chef Francis Mallmann; Lorenzo and Antonello; Melesio and Jason Momoa; Ignacio serves it up (Donna Lennard's personal archives); feeding the crowd, il Buco; Bernardo (Gentl & Hyers); Joel tending fire; Alberto and Roberto; Joaquin (all other photographs: Michael Grimm)

for the added flourish of your elegant illustrations. To our recipe tester, Sarah Karnasiewicz, and to my agent, Sarah Smith, at the David Black Agency. To our editor, Elinor Hutton, who jumped in just in time to shepherd this book to completion with her sheer grit, and the enormous support of Lynne Yeamans and the team at Harper Design, whose tremendous faith and dedication made this book possible.

To my dear friend and publicist, Jesse Gerstein and style-savvy Elizabeth Blitzer. To David and Monica Zwirner, who believed in the Alimentari dream, and to our first-class landlord, Anthony Lauto, who helped build it with the support of Luca Boniciolli, Grayling Design, and Howard Haimes. And to Steve Breskin and Jerry Atkins, who got the whole thing started on Bond Street in 1994 when they rented a little artist's showroom to a crazy Italian and his American girl.

To all the producers, artisans, distributors, and importers whose labor and craft inspire me constantly and allow me to deliver the best I can provide, day after day, and whose friendships are indelible. And to all my delicious guests and friends in the biz and outside of it who participated by sharing in these stories over the course of the journey and continue to share their creativity in this unprecedented moment in our industry and in our world.

This book belongs to all of you . . . with love.

—Donna Lennard

....

First, I'd like to thank Donna Lennard for letting me be part of this amazing journey. A journey it truly was. Then I'd like to thank my compatriots on the trip: Ocelot, Polar Bear, Gecko, Golden Retriever, and most importantly, Vampire Bat. During those two weeks in the summer of 2019, in the back of a van, amongst the olive trees of Umbria, on a street in Catania, on a beach in Ibiza, I felt all the love there is to feel in the world, and I won't forget that feeling.

Stateside, Harding Aldonzar was a beacon and a blessing of Bond Street. A block north, future Booker Prize winner Adjua Greaves, my favorite dungeon master Aubrey Jowers, the brother-in-mustache Kelvin Gonzalez, and Super-trooper Sherry Zuckerman were my guardian angels at Alimentari, always ready with an oat milk cortado and an egg sandwich to sustain me. Danny Rubin, thank you for being a mensch. Thank you to the Madson siblings too—Preston and Lauren—you two are both insane people in the best way. Sarah Karnasiewicz made sure these recipes actually worked, so we should all thank her. Dana Bowen and Pete Ferencevych at the Dynamite Shop kept me caffeinated and from being too lonely during the writing process. Thank you to Su Barber for making the book beautiful; Elinor Hutton, editorial pinch hitter, for bringing the book home; and to Rica Allannic and Sarah Smith of David Black Agency, for making sure it found one.

—Joshua David Stein

CLOCKWISE FROM TOP LEFT: Vendor, Catania fish market; roasted beets; fish, Scalia anchovies; John Derian, outside il Buco; Bevagna piazza; David Tanis leaves the greenmarket; Lauren Hutton with morning tea, Alimentari; coffee and pastries, Trapani

INDEX

Published in 2020 by
Harper Design
An Imprint of HarperCollins*Publishers*
195 Broadway
New York, NY 10007
Tel: (212) 207-7000
Fax: (855) 746-6023
harperdesign@harpercollins.com
www.hc.com

Distributed throughout the world by
HarperCollins Publishers
195 Broadway
New York, NY 10007

ISBN: 978-0-06-295838-9
Library of Congress Control Number: 2020029049

Excerpt from "Ode to Salt" by Pablo Neruda has
been reprinted with permission from the University
of California Press.

Design by Su Barber
Photography by Gentl & Hyers, with exceptions
as noted on pages x, 4, 5, 9, 10, 11, 13, 16, 298,
299, 300, and 301 by Noe DeWitt, Michael Grimm,
Thibault Jeansen, and Giada Paoloni
Edited by Elinor Hutton
Illustrations by Maya Netzer Horton
Prop styling by Ayesha Patel
Food styling by Susie Theodorou

Printed in Canada
First Printing, 2020